MAKING GREAT CONVERSATIONALISTS

STEVE AND TERI MAXWELL

Making Great Conversationalists

Ordering information:

Titus2, Inc.
1504 Santa Fe Street
Leavenworth, Kansas 66048
Phone: (913) 772-0392
Web site: Titus2.com

Published by:
Communication Concepts, Inc.
Web site: we-communicate.com

ACKNOWLEDGMENTS

Scripture taken from the HOLY BIBLE,
KING JAMES VERSION.

ISBN 978-0-9823003-8-1

Printed in the United States of America.

1

This book was created in Pages. InDesign CS6 and Adobe Photoshop were used for layout and design.

Joseph Maxwell designed the cover and interior.

TABLE OF CONTENTS

PREFACE

This book was conceived after many discussions our family had in the past ten years about the difficulty of having meaningful conversations with others. We realized this was because of a lack of conversation skills on the part of others. Additionally, a family told us they would love a resource they could use to teach their children the conversation skills they observed in our children. Finally, we had the direction of the Lord Jesus on our hearts that this was indeed the next writing project we should undertake.

If our children are to shine as lights to a dark world, they will need to be able to have conversations with those who don't know Jesus. "That ye may be blameless and harmless, the sons of God, without rebuke, in the midst of a crooked and perverse nation, among whom ye shine as lights in the world" (Philippians 2:15). They should stand out as different, and they also have to be able to articulate the reality of their faith. "But sanctify the Lord God in your hearts: and *be* ready always to *give* an answer to every man that asketh you a reason of the hope that is in you with meekness and fear" (1 Peter 3:15).

We are extremely excited about the potential for your children that you hold in your hands. We are praying that many will use this material with their children, and that it will profoundly impact their lives for good.

Our family affirmed this writing project and came alongside us with ideas for it and practical daily help to free up our time. In addition, they gave of the talents and skills the Lord has given them to make a few words on a computer screen become the reality of a published book.

Sarah invested hours proofreading the book both before and after the professional proofreader. Anna took the project from our Word file into the publishing software—a time consuming, detail-oriented task. Joseph is our creative element so he helped with choosing fonts, setting up styles for specific pages, and designing the cover. We also want to thank the six families who read this book, implemented it, and gave us feedback before it was printed.

We are very grateful to the Lord for the proof in our children's lives that what you read in these pages is important and valid. Plain and simply—it works!

Steve and Teri Maxwell

GOOD OR BAD CONVERSATIONS?

Have you ever taken a child to the grocery store and had this experience? A pleasant grandma looks at your five-year-old and tries to engage her in a conversation.

"Hello, sweetie. Those pigtails are just too cute. What's your name?"

Your child looks down at the floor and says nothing while you feel like melting into the floor yourself. However, you cheerfully attempt to prompt your child to answer.

"Tell the nice lady your name, honey."

No response. "Mommy said to tell her your name!"

Still no response so you continue to press. "You need to tell the lady your name!" By this point the grandma is looking decidedly embarrassed and obviously wishing she had not asked the little girl her name.

Finally, your daughter mutters under her breath, "Cynthia."

"What was that, my dear? I am sorry. I couldn't understand you," the grandma replies.

So you try again. "Speak up louder, and say your name clearly."

Again Cynthia says her name but still not so the lady can understand. You finally step in and tell her Cynthia's name.

That is a typical interaction for an adult with a five-year-old. It's what happens most of the time. How would you feel, though, if this were the way the conversation went instead?

"Hello, sweetie. Those pigtails are just too cute. What's your name?"

Your child looks at the grandma, smiles, and replies, "Thank you. My mommy likes to sometimes make pigtails for me. My name is Cynthia. What's your name?"

Impossible for a five-year-old, you say? We want to assure you that it is entirely possible, and through the information in this book, you will learn how to make those kinds of conversations a reality for your children.

ARE TEENS EQUIPPED TO CONVERSE EFFECTIVELY?

What about this scenario? You are missing work to take your fourteen-year-old son, Gerald, to the doctor because of a stomachache he has had for the last week. You and he have been waiting in silence for twenty minutes, and now the doctor comes into the examination room.

"Hi, Gerald, my name is Dr. Grote. What can I do for you today?"

Gerald looks at you as if you were going to answer, but you nod so Gerald says, "Well, my stomach hurts."

"How long has it bothered you?" Dr. Grote queries.

"Well, I'm not sure, ya know, ah, it's been awhile," Gerald manages.

"It's a week yesterday, Doc," you add.

"Show me where it hurts and describe the pain."

"Right here, and it really hurts. Ya know?" Your son shows the doctor where it hurts.

"Would you describe it as sharp, aching, cramping, or throbbing pain?"

"Umm, maybe, no, let's see. I guess I'd say sharp," Gerald half mutters.

"Did it start quickly or gradually?"

"I don't know for sure." At this point, you are wondering what Dr. Grote thinks of your parenting skills when your teenager can't respond to him any better than this.

Let's look at how the interaction could go if Gerald learns how to talk to others, answer questions, provide information, and carry on a conversation.

"Dad, I sure hope Dr. Grote will give me something for this stomachache. I really don't want to miss choir practice tomorrow night. I already missed last week's practice."

"Son, I hope so too. What songs are you learning in choir right now?"

Your father and son conversation goes on for the twenty-minute wait, and then Dr. Grote enters the room.

"Hi, Gerald, my name is Dr. Grote. What can I do for you today?"

"Well, sir, I've had this sharp pain in my stomach for the last week."

Dr. Grote nods and asks, "Why don't you lay back on the table here and point to exactly where it is hurting?"

"It's right here. It hurts the worst for about an hour after I eat. Then it is better, but it never really goes away. I have tried taking Tums for it, but that hasn't helped. My mom thought I should try the BRAT diet which was bananas, rice, applesauce, and toast. I did that for two days, but there wasn't any difference."

Gerald's interaction with Dr. Grote is one with which you could be pleased. He answers questions, gives extra useful information, and is easy to understand. The time before the doctor came into the room was profitable fellowship between you and your son.

We believe that if you will use this book to teach your children, they will become dynamic conversationalists. They will be able to comfortably interact with adults in the various situations in which they find themselves, just like Gerald did in his second conversation with the doctor.

WILL HE BE READY FOR THE COURTING CALL?

As our children get older, the stakes become higher and conversation failures more costly. Your twenty-three-year-old son, Rob, has a full-time job and knows a godly young lady whom he would like to court with the purpose of marriage. He knows the procedure is for the young man to approach the girl's father to express interest in his daughter. The big day for the all-important phone call has arrived.

Ring... Ring... "Hello. Dan Simmons here."

"Eh, yeah, ummm. This is Rob Miller calling. Do ya got a minute?"

"Sure, Rob, what's on your mind?"

"Well, uh, I'm, ah, well... I was, thinking, ah, well, and ah, like, ah, I need to talk to you."

"Rob, go ahead."

"Yeah, well, um, like, I, I, I really like Katie. Uh, can I court her?"

"Rob, that's a very important question. I would like to spend some time with you, get to know you, and then pray about that answer. I happen to have some time right now. Why don't we start getting to know each other? Tell me a little about yourself."

"Well, um, I'm twenty-three and have my own car."

"Anything else?"

"Well, um, I have three brothers and three sisters."

"And?"

"My dad is an electrician."

"Rob, why don't you tell me about yourself spiritually, what you do for a living, and what your interests are—those sorts of things."

"Sure, of course. Well, I like, ah, Mr. Simmons, I'm sort of nervous about this, you know?"

"Of course, Rob, I understand."

"Well, I'm twenty-three and have my own car. Oh, I think I told you that. Well, and ah, I work for Dan Harmon doing construction. I, and ah, I've worked for him like, two years now. And ah, let's see. I ah, joined the church when I was eight. And ah, I sang in the choir for like five years, and I go to the singles' group at church. Well, um, my interests? I, ah, like to work on my car a lot. Well, um, I suppose that's mostly it. Anything else you want to know?"

What is the likelihood of Mr. Simmons seriously considering your son as a candidate to court his daughter? If you were Mr. Simmons, might you have some serious questions as to whether Rob was capable of providing for and protecting your daughter simply by the way he handled this important conversation? What a poor impression Rob just made.

Now let's replay Rob's initial phone call as a good conversationalist because you have taught him necessary conversation skills. Notice how confident and smooth he is.

Ring... Ring... "Hello. Dan Simmons here."

"Mr. Simmons, this is Rob Miller calling. Do you have a minute, sir?"

"Sure, Rob. What's on your mind?"

"Mr. Simmons, I feel the Lord has been telling me that it is time to get married, and He keeps putting your daughter, Katie, on my heart as the one He wants for my wife. Sir, I wanted to share that with you, so that you might prayerfully consider my interest in courting Katie.

"I am sure you already know some things about me, but I would like to get together with you privately and explain what the Lord Jesus is doing in my life and how He is leading me. It would give you an opportunity to ask any questions you might have of me. Is there a convenient time we could get together?"

Did you notice how Rob performed this time? He confidently took charge of the call and clearly communicated his purpose. Mr. Simmon's initial opinion of Rob would have been that he was a young man who knew where he was going and conversed on an adult level. It is too early to tell whether Mr. Simmons would let Rob court Katie, but it is likely that Rob has succeeded in making a great impression.

Do you want to prepare your children for the important time in their lives when they will be entering a courtship or an engagement? Whether they are communicating with a future spouse or an in-law, the ability to converse will be vitally important to them. We believe the information in this book will help you equip your child for that critical time in his life.

WILL THEY BE PREPARED FOR MARRIED LIFE?

April and Ryan have been married for two years, and they have an eight-month-old baby. Ryan works for a telecommunications company that involves a half-hour commute to work while April stays home caring for baby Joseph.

At six-thirty, April hears the garage door go up, announcing Ryan's return home from work. She picks up Joseph and hurries down the stairs to greet him. "Ryan, I hope dinner isn't spoiled since you had to work late. It's your favorite—chicken enchiladas. I sure wish you could have come home on time. It's been a long day. Joseph has been extra fussy today, and he only took two half-hour naps all day! Because it was rainy, we couldn't even go for our morning walk. The day seemed so long, and now I have a terrible headache. I sure hope you are planning to spend some time with us tonight."

Ryan is checking his e-mails and text messages as he emerges from the car. "Sorry, April."

"Joseph wouldn't eat his sweet potatoes. He kept spitting them out. Then he took his cup and threw it on the floor every time I put it back on his high-chair tray. I think something is wrong with the washing machine. It is making a funny noise that I haven't heard before. I tried to write a check for the electric bill, but I couldn't find the checkbook. Do you know where it is?"

"No." Ryan hugs the two of them while reading his phone over their shoulders. "I really want to get changed. Why don't you put Joseph in his pack-n-play while you get dinner finished up?"

So many stay-at-home mommies with little children are starved for adult conversation when their husbands return home from work. Like many of them, April blasts Ryan with all the problems of the day, while he remains engaged in his work issues either mentally or through his phone. They are not building the kind of relationship they would like to have—a relationship that is developed through good conversation. Let's see how that conversation could have gone if both April and Ryan had learned to be loving conversationalists.

At six-thirty, April hears the garage door go up, announcing Ryan's return home from work. She picks up Joseph and hurries down the stairs to greet him. "Joseph, Daddy's home!" she bubbles to the baby as they move into the garage. "Ryan, I kept dinner warm in the oven since you had to work late. We have been so looking forward to having you home."

"Me too. It was a rough day at work. I will tell you all about it when we eat dinner. How was your day, sweetheart?"

"My day was rough too. I'll tell you more about that later. Would you believe Joseph sat up all by himself after his nap when he was playing on the floor? I hope he does it again tonight for you. He was so cute, and I actually think he looked proud of himself."

"Yeah! Another milestone for our little man," Ryan hugs the two of them and takes Joseph into his arms. "Hey, Joseph, Daddy loves you so much, and I am so happy to be home with you."

April says, "I made your favorite for dinner tonight. Chicken enchiladas. I'll go put the food on the table while you play with Joseph."

We believe you want to set your children on a path toward a solid marriage relationship. This book will allow you to teach your children the conversation skills that will facilitate that desire.

WERE THEY GOOD OR BAD?

These are just a few snippets of conversations from typical, daily life. They exemplify two very real possibilities for each conversation. What did you think of each one? Where would you fit with your conversation skills? What about your children?

We believe that parents would like their children to be equipped with dynamic conversation skills so that they are living out this verse. "Let your speech *be* alway with grace, seasoned with salt, that ye may know how ye ought to answer every man" (Colossians 4:6). We think it is very possible. Do you?

THE PRACTICAL SIDE

IN REAL LIFE

Just this past Sunday at church, I was out in the hall with my nine-year-old helping me with the two-year-old and three-month-old. While in the hall, another little nine-year-old girl, whom my daughter has met before, was also out there waiting for her older sister. I encouraged Shiloh, my daughter, to go and say hello to the other little girl. She didn't want to go over. The other little girl, also just as shy, stood there with her head down or walked in circles. I again encouraged Shiloh to go and say hello, giving her a few examples of things she could say or ask. Again, she did not want to go over. She claimed she was afraid and thought it silly to just walk over and say hello. Finally, at my pleading, she walked over and said hello. She told me later that her conversation went well; it was just getting over the fear of approaching the other little girl.

BOILING IT DOWN

Teach your children:

- There are good and bad conversations.
- They can choose which kind of conversations they want to have.

MAKING IT STICK

1. Read the good and bad conversations in this chapter as a family. Discuss them. Can your children discern the good ones from the bad ones? What do they think makes the good ones good and the bad ones bad?
2. Sit down individually with each child with the stated purpose to talk. Go somewhere private in the house where there won't be distractions. Tell the child you

want to talk with him, and let him know he isn't in trouble. Ask your child some questions and then evaluate his conversation with you. Here are some suggestions for questions you could ask. Ask if he has anything pressing that he has wanted to talk to you about. Ask if he is having any problems in general, any problems with you, or any problems with other family members. Ask him how he is spending his time.

3. After the discussion evaluate your child with the following questions. Make sure you write down your answers and any other pertinent information concerning your child's ability as a conversationalist so you can compare it to a conversation you will have with your child after finishing this book.
    - Were you able to spend fifteen minutes talking with the child?
    - Did conversation flow between you?
    - Was it give and take or one-sided?
    - Was it difficult to come up with conversation topics?
    - Did your child listen?
    - Did he seem interested?
    - Did he answer with a word or two or with whole sentences?
    - Did he ask you questions?

CHAPTER 2

WHAT IS A CONVERSATION?

Thirteen years ago the Lord opened a speaking ministry for our family. That meant travel and meeting many new people. Our youngest child was three at the time and our oldest, who wasn't married, was twenty. Those children were thrown into a conversation arena that provided many opportunities for developing conversation skills. We didn't have the teaching-conversation tools you now have, but we were aware of the importance of conversation skills, and we wanted our children to develop those skills. That meant we were discussing with our children how to talk to adults and children. We were encouraging them to initiate conversations and ask questions.

Not only did we coach our children, but our after-conference discussions were about the conversations that family members had experienced at the conferences. Then we had family evaluations of those conversations. Through trial and error, we learned and practiced what we are suggesting you do with your children.

As we write this book, those children who learned conversation through travel with us are sixteen to thirty-four, although the thirty-four-year-old has been married for two years and is no longer on the road with us. Our children have become those expert conversationalists we think you want your children to be.

Our children can make the loner feel like a part of the group. They can engage those who are difficult to talk to. They can listen attentively to the one who talks endlessly about himself. They can challenge. They can minister. They can edify. They can lead someone to the Lord. They do it through their conversations.

There is nothing spectacular about our children. One is very personable and is a natural conversationalist. However, the rest of us have had to work to develop conversation skills. We want to encourage you that if we can do it, you can do it!

IS CONVERSATION A PROBLEM?

Something else grew out of our travel, conferences, and personal conversations with those who attended our conferences. We became concerned about your children. This is a typical conversation one of our children would have at a conference with a young person of, perhaps, sixteen years old.

Our Anna would initiate the conversation. "Hi, my name is Anna."

"Hi," the new girl responds.

"What's your name?"

"Stacy."

"It's nice to meet you, Stacy. I'm so glad you were able to come to the conference. I hope you will like it and learn something from it. Where do you live?"

"Simpsonville."

"How far is that from here? I am not very familiar with the geography in this area because I am from Kansas."

"Don't know."

"What do you like to do, Stacy?"

"Read."

"Tell me about your favorite book."

"I don't have a favorite."

Through this conversation, Anna is working to engage Stacy. Sometimes Stacy looks at Anna, but other times she is looking around. Stacy halfway manages to answer Anna's questions, but she doesn't give more than basic information, and she never asks Anna a question. Two sixteen-year-old girls should be able to have a delightful conversation, perhaps a little like this:

Our Anna would initiate the conversation. "Hi, my name is Anna."

"Hi. My name is Stacy. I am excited to be at the conference with my family," the new girl responds.

"Why are you excited about it?" Anna asks.

"Our family has really been growing in the Lord lately. My dad shared some of the session titles and descriptions with us. They sounded really good. I especially liked the one about brothers and sisters. Do you have many brothers and sisters?" Stacy continues the conversation.

"I have two sisters and five brothers. It is from those relationships that the Lord has given us the material we share in the *Brothers and Sisters Best Friends Forever* session. How many siblings do you have, and what is your biggest struggle with them?"

When we realized that a good conversation was the exception rather than the rule, we decided that maybe we could assist parents in doing what is most important to them—helping their children.

DOES YOUR FAMILY COMMUNICATE OR CONVERSE?

We will be using the word "conversation" many times in this book, so we will define it here. Conversation is a verbal exchange of information between two or more people.

Just as an artist creates beautiful pictures that please the eyes, those skillful in conversation provide appropriate, flowing words. Whether it is for encouragement, exhortation, comfort, or edification, they are the right words for the circumstance. "A word fitly spoken *is like* apples of gold in pictures of silver" (Proverbs 25:11).

Recently we were at an oral surgeon's office who was going to remove our son's wisdom teeth. Jesse and I (Steve) were escorted into an examining room and instructed where to sit. The assistant turned on a DVD that played for ten minutes, telling us all about wisdom teeth removal and follow-up care. Next the surgeon came in and began telling Jesse about the procedure and certain things we should know.

To this point, it was not a conversation but communication. Communication is much broader in scope than conversation. Communication is the giving or receiving of information such as thoughts, opinions, or facts via speech or writing, whether electronically or by other means. Examples of communication are speaking, writing, preaching, and teaching. Communication is far more global than conversation.

To this point in the pre-surgery appointment, they were strictly giving us information, first via the DVD and then in person as the oral surgeon recited facts that he had repeated many times before. There was no exchange back from us other than to indicate we understood what they wanted us to know. We were interested in what we were hearing because it would impact Jesse's health. It was neither enjoyable nor awkward—just the passing of information.

However, after the medical part was completed, the surgeon transformed from a sterile doctor into a conversationalist. He asked Jesse some questions about himself, and the flow of information went both ways. We entered into a conversation.

Jesse and I asked him questions on a personal level, and he in turn asked us more. He asked about Jesse's school and future plans. He asked about what I did for a living and where we went to church, among other topics. We were able to ask him some questions and learn a bit about his life, including his love for going on medical mission trips to Haiti. For over twenty minutes we carried on a conversation. When the communication turned into an enjoyable conversation, it no longer was cold and dry communication but a pleasurable, relationship-building experience. He was a warm, caring person who had a heart for his patients.

As a father at that moment, I was grateful that my sixteen-year-old son had learned the art of conversation. When the oral surgeon asked Jesse questions, he spoke up and articulated his answers. Not only was Jesse able to do that, but he was also able to continue the conversation by asking the doctor questions. That skill will be a tool Jesse will use throughout his life.

DO YOU WANT TO HELP YOUR CHILDREN?

Do you have a sincere desire to help your children learn conversation skills? This might begin with your own learning or improving your conversation abilities. We think everyone has room for growth in this area. If we will acknowledge to the Lord that we would like to improve our conversation skills so as to be better used by Him, then we can be encouraged that improvement is possible both for us and for our children. "And this is the confidence that we have in him, that, if we ask any thing according to his will, he heareth us: And if we know that he hear us, whatsoever we ask, we know that we have the petitions that we desired of him" (1 John 5:14-15).

If we ask Him to help us teach our children those skills as well, we will have the power of His Spirit aiding our efforts. "I can do all things through Christ which strengtheneth me" (Philippians 4:13).

Of course, we can't ask the Lord Jesus for help learning to be a better conversationalist or teaching our children how to converse if we don't have a relationship with Him. He must be our Savior in order for Him to answer our prayers. "The LORD *is* far from the wicked: but he heareth the prayer of the righteous" (Proverbs 15:29). If you aren't sure about your salvation, we would encourage you to go to Chapter 12 where you will find information on how to be saved and you can read Steve and Teri's testimony in Appendix E.

HOW DO YOU USE THIS BOOK?

This book is designed for parents so they can learn how to teach their children to be excellent conversationalists. At the end of each chapter, you will find a section called "Boiling It Down." These chapter highlights will be useful and important to you as you instruct your children in conversation skills. These notes are the points you will use to teach your children about conversation.

There are also sections at the end of each chapter called "Making It Stick" that are assignments for your family that will give an opportunity for practice and evaluation. To get the most out of your investment of time, be sure to work through each exercise.

In a notebook or a computer document, write down the answers to the questions and make notes about each assignment. This will track your experience so that you will be able to look back over time, see change, and be encouraged by your progress.

The "In Real Life" portions of the chapters are snippets of child conversationalists in real-life situations. They were shared with us by families who read this material when it was still in draft form.

We want you to catch a glimpse of the practicality of what you are reading to motivate you to do what it takes to make conversation progress with your children.

CAN YOUR CHILDREN IMPROVE?

Families are in a conversation crisis! They spend their time watching TV or movies. They are glued to their computers and smart phones. Texting and e-mail has eliminated many opportunities for conversation. They are so on-the-go that they seldom have meals together. We think families should spend time together conversing and learning to be proficient conversationalists.

Every one of us can improve our conversation skills from Dad down to a toddler. One dad who read this book told us after reading it:

> *"I felt convicted and realized that I am way more of a communicator than I am a conversationalist. I wish I had read this much earlier in life. I feel that my relationships would have been broader and richer if I had. I love the idea of using this material to teach my children because I can definitely see room for improvement. I believe the stories and exercises will help each member of my family."*

A person who comes in contact with a non-conversationalist can find himself wishing to move on to someone else who is easier and more pleasant to talk to. We don't want our children to be those people whom others avoid because they are difficult to converse with. Therefore let's be determined to equip our children with necessary and adequate conversation skills.

Whether it is a young child interacting with a stranger in a store, a teen talking to his doctor, a young man wanting to start a courtship, or a married couple, we can prepare our children to be successful in these normal, everyday interactions that they will encounter. Some will be inconsequential, mundane conversations, but others will be life-changing ones.

It is the goal of this book to help you as a parent know how to teach your children to have great conversations. One might think good conversation skills are naturally acquired as children learn to talk and mature. However, that does not appear to be the case. Confirm that to yourself by evaluating the conversations you are involved in and those you hear around you.

There is an equipping process that we can step our children through to teach them how to have a quality conversation. Instruction, practice, and evaluation will be part of the package. Are you ready?

We are very excited about the potential these pages have for impacting the lives of your children and generations to come after them. Be encouraged that as you progress through this book, and apply yourself to the material, not only will your conversation skills improve but you will be equipped to teach them to your children. Let's get started!

THE PRACTICAL SIDE

IN REAL LIFE

1. Our children were able to build a very good friendship

with our mailman, Mr. Don. It started off with him asking questions and getting one word answers from our children. Once we (the parents) established that Mr. Don was a Christian man and one that was "safe" for the children to talk to and give more personal information, often the children waited by the mailbox to talk to Mr. Don. He was very good at remembering each of their names and asking about their school subjects and what they were doing. Soon the children were able to ask him questions as well. He would even send them postcards when he went on vacation!

2. This past week we had to take our nine-year-old daughter, Shiloh, to the doctor. She and her brother had run into each other, causing Shiloh's teeth to go into her lip. It had become infected, so we needed to see the doctor. Before leaving, Mom was able to walk through a possible conversation with our doctor with Shiloh. She was able to give Shiloh guidance in being able to thoroughly tell the doctor what happened, how her lip was feeling, and what we had been doing before we came to see him. At the appointment, Shiloh spoke clearly and was able to explain in detail all about the accident and what was going on with her lip currently. She did a very good job of communicating why she was there to see him.

BOILING IT DOWN

Teach your children:

- Conversation is a verbal exchange of information between two or more people.
- They can learn to be good conversationalists.

MAKING IT STICK

1. Give everyone who is old enough to write a piece of paper. Read the following questions and have them record their answers.
    1. As a conversationalist rate yourself. _____ (1 poor, 10 excellent)
    2. Rate your conversation with the following people: (1 poor, 10 excellent)
        - Friends _____
        - Strangers _____
        - Spouse _____
        - Children _____
        - Parent _____
        - Siblings _____
    3. Do you have any fears in talking with others? What are they?
    4. Do you have a "technique" for speaking with someone new? If so, what is it?

5. Do you normally choose to speak with others your age?
6. Are you confident in sharing the Gospel with the lost?
7. Are there any things that annoy you about other people's conversation skills? What are they?
8. What do you think are key factors in someone being a good conversationalist? (Think of someone you enjoy talking to. What does that person do that makes it enjoyable?)
9. After a conversation with someone new to you, do you generally come away feeling you have learned a great deal about them?
10. Do you want to improve in your conversation skills?
11. Do you want your children to improve their conversation skills?

2. After answering the questions, go through each question and have everyone discuss their answers. Do you all agree with how each rated himself?
3. Read the good and bad conversation at the beginning of this chapter as a family. Discuss it. Can your children discern the good one from the bad one? What do they think makes the good one good and the bad one bad?

ARE CONVERSATION SKILLS IMPORTANT?

Mrs. Monroe has just brought a plate of cookies to Mrs. Jones' house to welcome the Joneses to the neighborhood.

"May I help you?" asks Mrs. Jones as she opens the door.

"I'm Mrs. Monroe from next door, and I wanted to welcome you to the neighborhood."

"That is so kind and thoughtful of you. We just moved in yesterday, and the house is a mess or I'd invite you in," Mrs. Jones responds.

"Well, I—" Mrs. Monroe starts to comment, but Mrs. Jones interrupts her.

"We've had this to fix and that. It is amazing how much work this house has taken. We thought it was in good shape, but were we ever wrong. We've already called the plumber and electrician. Let me tell you, they were expensive," continues Mrs. Jones.

"I'm sorry. Have you tried—" Mrs. Monroe makes another attempt to be part of the conversation.

"I've even got a call into the air conditioning man and am expecting him to get back to me any minute. Do you have any idea how hot it is in our house? It feels like it could be almost one hundred degrees, and it is only eleven o'clock. I can only guess how hot it will be this afternoon. I tried to open the windows, but I couldn't get any of them to open. Those are two more repairmen I will need to call. I think those calls should be my husband's responsibility. I don't know why he isn't the one making them. He can deal with these people much better than I can. Oh, yes, and thank you for the cookies. I must be going. Nice talking with you. Stop by anytime. Bye," says Mrs. Jones as she steps back inside the house.

"Bye," replies Mrs. Monroe.

What kind of relationship did this conversation generate between these two ladies? How likely is it that Mrs. Monroe will ever try to visit with Mrs. Jones again? Let's see if the outcome would have been different had Mrs. Jones been a good conversationalist.

DO YOU LIKE THE CHANGE?

Mrs. Monroe has just brought a plate of cookies to Mrs. Jones' house to welcome the Joneses into the neighborhood.

"May I help you?" asks Mrs. Jones as she opens the door.

"I'm Mrs. Monroe from next door, and I wanted to welcome you to the neighborhood," Mrs. Monroe smiles as she hands Mrs. Jones the cookies.

"That is so kind and thoughtful of you. Thank you. We just moved in yesterday, and there isn't even a place to sit down, or I'd invite you in. But I would love to take a minute and hear about your family," Mrs. Jones replies.

"Well, Bob and I have been married twelve years, and God has blessed us with four children so far. The children range from age ten down to three, and we are expecting another one in August. Tell me about your family," Mrs. Monroe answers.

"Jim and I have been married for twenty-four years and have two children. Daniel is twenty, and Melissa is seventeen. We've homeschooled them since the beginning," responds Mrs. Jones.

"Really? Homeschooled? You must have so much patience. I don't think I could ever homeschool. I'm just not patient enough," Mrs. Monroe says.

What a difference! This is the kind of conversation that builds friendships—a great beginning for these two neighbors.

DOES CONVERSATION AFFECT RELATIONSHIPS?

Remember that conversation is communication between two or more people. It is a necessary part of social interaction that establishes and deepens relationships. The purpose of speech is not to fill silence.

The goal of conversation is to be a mutually enjoyable exchange of information between people for the goal of edification. "Let no corrupt communication proceed out of your mouth, but that which is good to the use of edifying, that it may minister grace unto the hearers" (Ephesians 4:29).

Relationships are going to be a key component in your child's future. Solid, strong relationships will make his life fulfilling and enjoyable. The more conversations we have with someone, the greater potential there is in developing a relationship with him. For example, courtships involve many conversations between the courting couple. The more they talk and share deep heart feelings, the closer they become emotionally. In general, relationships will be either enhanced or degraded based on the quality of the conversations within them.

Because of conversation's importance in relationships, learning to communicate well is key to a life used by the Lord Jesus Christ. The better we can converse with people, the more potential we have of enjoying good relationships. "Pleasant words *are as* an honeycomb, sweet to the soul, and health to the bones" (Proverbs 16:24). We can significantly improve our children's lives by helping them learn to be good conversationalists. We find that very exciting! There are not many things a parent can do that don't cost a penny but can have such a dramatic impact on improving our children's lives and their futures!

The first chapter provided several examples of conversations. We "listened" to a very awkward and uncomfortable dialog between a son, Rob, and Dan Simmons about courting Dan's daughter, Katie. We hurt for Rob as he stammered and sputtered while hoping to make a good impression on Mr. Simmons. We kept wanting to give Rob a few hints on what to say and what might ease his misery.

How wonderful it was when we saw the other Rob, who had learned how to be a good conversationalist in the next dialog. We felt like cheering him on and saying, "Yeah, Rob! That's the way to show Mr. Simmons you would be a great son-in-law. Way to go!" His conversational skills were paving the way to a relationship with a future wife and father-in-law. Isn't that the preparation you would like to give your children?

Time on Earth is too short to waste. "Redeeming the time, because the days are evil" (Ephesians 5:16). Each one needs to be a highly effective conversationalist whom God can use to build strong, lasting relationships with others. It begins within a family, then moves on to neighbors, and also involves those with whom we do business and those with whom we worship. Instead of your child feeling uncomfortable or even dreading conversations, he can come to the place of greatly enjoying them, and being skillful in keeping the conversation alive and interesting to both parties involved.

Conversation is how one bridges the gap between two ships passing in the night. It is the spark that kindles warmth between two separate entities. "The lips of the righteous feed many: but fools die for want of wisdom" (Proverbs 10:21). As we drive through a city, there are cars everywhere with people in those cars all going somewhere. The reason we don't have relationships with all the people we see in other cars is that we haven't had the opportunity to engage them in conversations. At times there might be communication that goes on when one driver blasts his horn at another, but that sort of communication does not build relationships. It hinders them. "An angry man stirreth up strife, and a furious man aboundeth in transgression" (Proverbs 29:22).

HOW WILL CONVERSATION IMPROVE FAMILY RELATIONSHIPS?

One might consider that the smallest example of a city is a family. The members of a family can have deep relationships with each other, or they can be similar to those busy cars passing at intersections. The family members all reside in one location, but if they are busy going to and fro, they are not involved in each other's lives.

Within your family, how much do you really know about your children? How much do they know about you? How much do they know about their siblings? Does each love the others enough to open up his life to his family? "This is my commandment, That ye love one another, as I have loved you" (John 15:12).

Relationships within the family are highly dependent on the quality and substance of every member's ability to converse with the other family members. If someone in the family is withdrawn and won't talk, there will be a wall between him and the rest of the family. Offenses will accumulate and bitterness will likely result, building a taller and wider separation. "Looking diligently lest any man fail of the grace of God; lest any root of bitterness springing up trouble *you*, and thereby many be defiled" (Hebrews 12:15).

When everyone in the family is conversing freely, offenses can be dealt with quickly and easily. "Therefore if thou bring thy gift to the altar, and there rememberest that thy brother hath ought against thee; Leave there thy gift before the altar, and go thy way; first be reconciled to thy brother, and then come and offer thy gift" (Matthew 5:23-24). Each is able to understand the other better because there is an expression of needs and feelings.

Husband and wife are united in marriage. They are one before God and man, yet conversation will greatly determine how united in soul and spirit they are and how good the marriage is. For them to be one in soul, it takes ongoing, quality conversations. They must share deeply and frequently from the depth of their souls with each other.

A healthy marriage is similar to the need for our brain to be constantly "dialoging" with the different parts of the body. Our nerves pass information back and forth between our brain and our body. The operation of the body and our health depends on this. In the same way, if conversation between husband and wife is hindered, that relationship will degrade over time and could eventually fail. "Nevertheless let every one of you in particular so love his wife even as himself; and the wife *see* that she reverence *her* husband" (Ephesians 5:33). Look at the blessing you give your children's future marriages if you teach them how to have meaningful conversations.

Conversation is essential in discipling and training children. "My son, attend to my words; incline thine ear unto my sayings" (Proverbs 4:20). Children must be shown God's way and given an understanding of the way He desires that they live. It isn't sufficient to explain godly behavior once and expect there to be no further dialog. "And these words, which I command thee this day, shall be in thine heart: And thou shalt teach them diligently unto thy children..." (Deuteronomy 6:6-7).

Changing the course of a life away from the world's path will take ongoing quality discussions with each child in the family. "My son, keep my words, and lay up my commandments with thee" (Proverbs 7:1). Are you prepared to do this with your children? Will they be prepared to do it with their children?

Siblings can become each other's best friends when they learn to converse freely with each other. Time together and the talking that ensues build those relationships. "Behold, how good and how pleasant *it is* for brethren to dwell together in unity!" (Psalms 133:1). Friends will come and go, but when we cultivate our children being best friends, especially through their conversations, those relationships can last for a lifetime.

WILL CONVERSATION IMPROVE FRIENDSHIPS?

There is an old saying that says "variety is the spice of life." We believe that as you look at your days, you might agree that conversations are key to providing that variety. Often our discussions with people make one day more unique and spice it up when compared to another.

"Hey Bob, I haven't seen you in a long time. How's it going?"

"It's been crazy."

"Really? Why is that?" Andy questions.

"My uncle had his house heavily damaged by a tornado last month, and thankfully none of the family were injured. We've been driving three hours each weekend to help them repair their house. We stay with my grandma and go to church there. I've missed being home on the weekends, but it has been so good to help them."

"Whew! I understand now. Bless you all for helping your uncle like that," Andy encourages.

Here's another conversation.

"Hi Ashley. How are you?" Amy asks.

"I'm really good. I have exciting news!"

"What's that?"

"I just started a courtship with Chad Swisher. My dad has been talking to him for months, and I never knew it. Dad just told me last night and asked if I wanted to enter a courtship with Chad."

"Ashley, I'm so happy for you. This will be a very exciting time for you and Chad. I'll add you to my prayer journal. I'd love to hear the whole story," Amy replies.

Conversations open up a window into another's life. The quality and length of the conversation determines how wide that window is open. Our children's conversations with others will give spice to each day. Many spend precious time reading novels or watching movies, but conversations are true life, not made-up fiction. We are able to talk to real people with real adventures, real needs, real hurts, and real joys. Conversations are wonderful opportunities to get a mind off itself and onto others.

A mother at home all day with only an infant often longs for the time Dad comes home so she can have some meaningful dialog with him. When Dad arrives, what does he normally share? He tells Mom about interesting conversations and experiences he had during the day. In exchange, Mom will tell about her day. If there have been conversations with others, they will be shared, in addition to how it went with the baby.

Children enjoy play times, but even for them, it's the conversations with their playmates that make the time far more enjoyable. Children are known to tell all the family secrets. Why? Because they want to make the talk exciting for the one listening.

WILL CONVERSATION IMPROVE SUCCESS IN BUSINESS?

Most businesses' success is dependent on the staff being able to communicate with their customers. Even in an Internet business there will be phone calls to answer and relationships with suppliers to be developed and maintained. If our children aren't able to converse well with others in the business world, they will be severely challenged. The more outgoing, friendly, and able to carry on a great conversation the owner and employees are, the more a business will potentially thrive.

There was a franchise sandwich shop in our town, and for this example let's refer to it as Mr. Smart Cents. There was another franchise sandwich shop about a block away, and I will refer to that one as Goodway. Mr. Smart Cents was a small restaurant in a strip shopping center with only a few tables. If you wanted lunch there, you needed to arrive early or late to miss the lunch crowd because there was also minimal parking. Plus you could wait in line quite a while to get your sandwich and then not be able to find an open table. If you couldn't get in at Mr. Smart Cents, you could go across the street to Goodway. There was always parking and seating room there. One might wonder why one shop was so much more popular than the other even though they seemed to have comparable products. I have a good guess, and I will share it with you.

At Mr. Smart Cents, the owner was there interacting with the customers. You could expect a cheerful, "How are you today?" or "Good to see you!" Sometimes he would take orders, but other times he would just greet customers and speak with them. He was so friendly and outgoing that he made you feel welcome. You thought you were visiting an old friend every time you went into his sandwich shop. Sadly, at Goodway, the owner was absent, and the employees were unfriendly. If you were hungry and just wanted something in your stomach, Goodway would do, but if you wanted an enjoyable sandwich experience, you went to Mr. Smart Cents. That's what many people did. The spice that sweetened the visit was pleasant conversation, which made each guest feel important and welcome, bringing their business back frequently.

HOW WILL CONVERSATION HELP NEW RELATIONSHIPS?

Conversation opens a book from which our children can learn. Each person has a story within him that is a closed book until opened.

Recently, I (Steve) had to pick up some items at an electrical supply store. It was just before closing, and there was only one guy manning the shop. I hadn't seen him before, and so I didn't know anything about him.

I pointed to a product on the shelf behind him and questioned, "Is that a miniature camera on the pegboard?"

He replied, "No, but I know what you are talking about. My twenty-year-old daughter drives race cars, and she wants me to buy her a camera to mount on her helmet. I just haven't spent the money yet."

I noticed the way his face lit up when he mentioned his daughter and her racing. That was the beginning of a good conversation. In a short amount of time, I learned about his daughter, her racing history, and her current racing activities. I especially learned that this was a dad who deeply loved and invested his time and resources into his daughter's life. I now have an open door into his life when we continue the discussion in the future. We both had a wonderful time talking to each other, and I have a new friend!

Conversation is the key that will enable our children to sample the rich experiences of another's life. Each and every individual is precious enough that the Lord Jesus would have died for that person singularly. Conversation is a door into that life. We will never regret developing our children's conversation skills.

HOW WILL CONVERSATION SKILLS HELP IN BEING SALT AND LIGHT?

We are called to be "salt and light" to the lost and invite them to come to the Kingdom of Heaven through Jesus Christ. "Ye are the salt of the earth: but if the salt have lost his savour, wherewith shall it be salted? it is thenceforth good for nothing, but to be cast out, and to be trodden under foot of men. Ye are the light of the world. A city that is set on an hill cannot be hid" (Matthew 5:13-14). Do we truly love people and desire to introduce them to the King of kings and Lord of lords—Jesus Christ? If so, we will come to see that good conversational skills are critical to being properly equipped as a soldier of the Lord, and we will be key in that preparation for our children.

Our children can also be salt and light to the world as they introduce others to Christian thinking by what they talk about and how they share it. Many of those in the world have never been exposed to the truths of godliness and holiness, yet deep in their hearts, they have a yearning for purity and goodness.

Recently sixteen-year-old Mary and I (Teri) were returning a couple of items to Sam's Club. The customer-service lady looked at Mary and asked her, "What grade are you in?"

Mary responded, "Tenth grade."

"Where are you going to go to college?" the lady asked.

"I am not planning to go to college. I would like to be a wife and mother someday. In the meantime, I am studying art so I can illustrate children's books. I can do that at home and save all the money that college costs while not being exposed to the negative influences of college."

The grandmotherly customer-service lady seemed a little surprised, but Mary had presented her case so well that her only reply was, "That's nice."

In a short conversation, Mary was able to clearly state her goals for her life and persuasively speak against the customary thinking that young people should go to college. She gave a very different view to this woman than what the lady was probably used to hearing.

Conversation skills are necessary to be a leader, to be a follower, to be a comforter, to be an encourager, and to be an admonisher. It is one thing to know what to say in those examples, but if we aren't able to appropriately converse with others, it is like trying to hang wallpaper with both arms tied behind our backs. We may have the knowledge to do the job, but we can't implement what we need to do. Are our children equipped for these tasks?

WILL YOUR CHILDREN'S CONVERSATION SKILLS GET STRONGER?

Conversation skills are critical in life. When children learn these skills early, they have an advantage over others who don't have these skills. As we saw from the example between Rob and Mr. Simmons, if young men can't converse well with adults, they will likely have more trouble finding a wife. When speaking with young ladies, they also need to be good conversationalists. It would be the same for the daughter when she is interacting with a young man who is interested in courting her. If she can't carry on a conversation, how will their relationship grow?

Relationships in church and with neighbors are all dependent on our ability to converse well. In relationships, misunderstandings can crop up easily, and if we aren't skilled in conversing with others, those relationships will suffer.

By now you should have a deep appreciation for how important it is to be able to converse well. Anyone can become a skilled conversationalist by understanding some basic principles, having the right heart attitudes, and then practicing. Your children will become more comfortable and effective the more they practice. The best place to learn is at home, and then we experiment with others.

If we desire stronger muscles, we will begin by working them. In the same way, we have written conversation exercises that will help you begin to develop your children's conversation muscles. It is important that you work through the exercises. There are no shortcuts to becoming skilled. Now it's time to exercise.

THE PRACTICAL SIDE

IN REAL LIFE

When our family goes to the park, our children are to introduce themselves to the other children who are there. We usually go to the park when it is not crowded, so normally, there are only one or two other families there. If our children decide to play chase or hide-n-seek, they are to ask the other children if they would like to play. Finally, when we leave, our children approach the other children and say good-bye.

BOILING IT DOWN

Teach your children:

- The goal of conversation is to be a mutually enjoyable exchange of information between people for the goal of edification. "Let no corrupt communication proceed out of your mouth, but that which is good to the use of edifying, that it may minister grace unto the hearers" (Ephesians 4:29).

- The more conversations they have with someone, the greater potential there is in developing that relationship with him.

- Because of conversation's importance in relationships, learning to communicate well is key to a life used by the Lord Jesus Christ.

- Relationships within the family are highly dependent on the quality and substance of every member's ability to converse with the other family members.

- Conversations open up windows into others' lives.

- The more outgoing, friendly, and able to carry on a great conversation the owner and employees are, the more a business will potentially thrive.

- Conversations open books for learning.

- Good conversational skills are critical to being properly equipped as a soldier of the Lord. "Ye are the salt of the earth: but if the salt have lost his savour, wherewith shall it be salted? it is thenceforth good for nothing, but to be cast out, and to be trodden under foot of men. Ye are the light of the world. A city that is set on an hill cannot be hid" (Matthew 5:13-14).

- Conversation skills are necessary to be a leader, to be a follower, to be a comforter, to be an encourager, and to be an admonisher.

MAKING IT STICK

1. Read aloud and discuss as a family the conversations in this chapter.

WHAT ARE THE INGREDIENTS OF A GOOD CONVERSATION?

John walks into the living room where his dad is reading e-mail on his phone.

"Dad?"

"What?" John's dad responds still looking at his phone.

"I've been having trouble with Cathy. Lots of times she is saying things that aren't nice to me, and that bothers me."

"Hmmm." Dad glances at his son and then back to the phone.

"When I come out of the bathroom, she says I'm taking too much time. I only stay in as long as I need to, though. Yesterday she saw my jacket on the floor and told me I was a messy little kid. I dropped it there because Mom had told me to hurry to dinner. I was planning to hang it up later."

"Well," Dad mutters, still reading on his phone.

"I guess this isn't a good time to talk," John says as he dejectedly walks away.

John's dad lost a wonderful opportunity to demonstrate his love for his son by meaningfully sharing in this conversation with him.

WHAT IS THE MOTIVE FOR CONVERSATION?

The motive for good conversation needs to be love. When we love another, we have an attitude toward the other person that desires their best. Look at 1 Corinthians 13:4-7, the verses about love:

"Charity suffereth long, *and* is kind; charity envieth not; charity vaunteth not itself, is not puffed up, Doth not behave itself unseemly, seeketh not her own, is not easily provoked, thinketh no evil; Rejoiceth not in iniquity, but rejoiceth in the truth; Beareth all things, believeth all things, hopeth all things, endureth all things."

Consider how these loving attitudes will affect conversations. Let's go back to John for a specific example.

John walks into the room where his dad is reading e-mail on his phone.

"Dad?"

"Yes, son?" John's dad responds putting his phone back in its holder.

"I've been having trouble with Cathy. Lots of times she is saying things that aren't nice to me, and that bothers me."

"What kind of things does she say?" Dad asks looking intently at his son.

"When I come out of the bathroom, she says I'm taking too much time. I only stay in as long as I need to, though. Yesterday she saw my jacket on the floor and told me I was a messy little kid. I dropped it there because Mom had told me to hurry to dinner. I was planning to hang it up later."

"How do you think the Lord would have you respond to those comments?" John's dad asks him.

Their conversation continues with some deep, heartfelt sharing, and practical, spiritual instruction between father and son.

When John's dad put down his phone, looked at his son, and listened, he communicated love to John. In the conversation that followed, John's father was being long-suffering because there were other things he could have accomplished with that time. However, he set those plans aside to have a conversation with his son. He was kind by giving attention to John, and he certainly wasn't self-seeking since he was choosing to invest in John's life rather than reading his e-mails. We could go through each of the facets of the 1 Corinthians 13 basis for love to see how John's dad's conversation demonstrated them, but we think you have the idea.

WHAT IS THE FOUNDATION OF CONVERSATION?

As we teach our children about conversation, we will be instructing them that the foundation for conversation is love. "Beloved, let us love one another: for love is of God; and every one that loveth is born of God, and knoweth God" (1 John 4:7). We will continually remind them that as they work on conversation skills and engage others in conversation, they are demonstrating the love that Jesus Christ asks His children to show one another. It is likely we will need to help them learn to love as 1 Corinthians 13 encourages us to love and to have those qualities of love be evident in their conversations. "My son, hear the instruction of thy father, and forsake not the law of thy mother" (Proverbs 1:8).

Surely all of us have attempted to speak with someone who was preoccupied and unwilling to give us their attention, similar to John's father's initial response to him. It is easy to be self-focused and ignore the needs of those around us. I'm sure the frustration we felt reading the first account of John and his father was similar to John's frustration, and that is bad for a relationship. John did not feel valued or loved by his dad when his dad was not willing to put his phone aside and listen to him. How easy it is for us to instruct our children that they should give others their direct attention in a conversation, but it is far more important for us to model it for them. It starts with our example.

Do you remember the first conversation between Mrs. Jones and Mrs. Monroe and how Mrs. Jones kept talking? She wasn't interested in Mrs. Monroe. She was demonstrating a proud, self-focused heart that didn't appear to care for her new neighbor. "For he flattereth himself in his own eyes, until his iniquity be found to be hateful" (Psalms 36:2).

We need to help our children see how they can demonstrate love through conversations. "*Be* kindly affectioned one to another with brotherly love; in honour preferring one another" (Romans 12:10).

WHAT IS PARAMOUNT TO CONVERSATION?

Obedience to God's Word in our children's lives produces powerful conversations. "Thy word *is* a lamp unto my feet, and a light unto my path" (Psalms 119:105). Our children will stand or fall upon the foundation of the Word, so their lives must be consistent with the power of a sanctified life. Their words will be the "Amen" to their lives.

Because words come from the heart, our children need to have pure hearts or else their conversations are nothing but hypocrisy. "An hypocrite with *his* mouth destroyeth his neighbour: but through knowledge shall the just be delivered" (Proverbs 11:9).

"A good man out of the good treasure of his heart bringeth forth that which is good; and an evil man out of the evil treasure of his heart bringeth forth that which is evil: for of the abundance of the heart his mouth speaketh" (Luke 6:45). Pure hearts are obviously part of the outcome of the instruction we find in Ephesians 6:4 to "bring them up in the nurture and admonition of the Lord." To help our children develop lives that produce pure conversations, we should be in a continual discipleship process with them.

Our children's relationship with Christ is preeminent, and confessing Jesus as their Savior is critical. "That if thou shalt confess with thy mouth the Lord Jesus, and shalt believe in thine heart that God hath raised him from the dead, thou shalt be saved. For with the heart man believeth unto righteousness; and with the mouth confession is made unto salvation" (Romans 10:9-10). While that confession happens at salvation, it is also an ongoing process as our children regularly confess Christ through their conversations. Those words they share may mean the difference between heaven and hell for the others in the conversation.

WHERE IS THE POWER IN CONVERSATION?

We want our children to understand the power in the Word of God not only for their lives, but also for the lives of others. When they use God's Word, their conversations take on a higher level of authority and persuasiveness.

"Speaking to yourselves in psalms and hymns and spiritual songs, singing and making melody in your heart to the Lord" (Ephesians 5:19).

"Let the word of Christ dwell in you richly in all wisdom; teaching and admonishing one another in psalms and hymns and spiritual songs, singing with grace in your hearts to the Lord" (Colossians 3:16).

Let's listen to a snippet of conversation between two fourteen-year-olds whose families are having an evening of dinner and fellowship together.

"Susi, I am concerned about the way you treated your little sister by telling her she needed to go play somewhere else. The Bible says, 'And be ye kind one to another, tenderhearted, forgiving one another, even as God for Christ's sake hath forgiven you' (Ephesians 4:32). I really don't think you were being kind or tenderhearted to her."

"You're right, Emily. I was being selfish. All day she has been messing up whatever I'm involved with and making a lot of noise. I didn't want that to happen again. It would be better, though, to let her be with us."

"Maybe, Susi, we could find something for her to do. Let's go to the toy closet to see what we can find and invite her back."

Emily's conversation is more powerful than most children's conversations because she has a Bible verse to share. It should be more effective than it would have been just to tell her friend that she was being mean to her little sister. Teaching our children the Word, using it in our conversations with them, and encouraging them to use it in their conversations with others will enhance those conversations and relationships.

"For the word of God *is* quick, and powerful, and sharper than any twoedged sword, piercing even to the dividing asunder of soul and spirit, and of the joints and marrow, and *is* a discerner of the thoughts and intents of the heart" (Hebrews 4:12).

"All scripture *is* given by inspiration of God, and *is* profitable for doctrine, for reproof, for correction, for instruction in righteousness: That the man of God may be perfect, throughly furnished unto all good works" (2 Timothy 3:16-17).

For our children to be able to utilize Scripture in their conversations, we should have them memorize Scripture, and show them appropriate places for a verse or a reference to a biblical story to be used. It helps if we use the Word in our conversations. Then it will flow more naturally from the child's mouth as well.

God knows the power of His Word and of words in general. That is why there are so many verses in Scripture instructing us on proper speech. Of the 915 verses in Proverbs, about one-third of them have to do with our words and how words are to be used. Here are a couple of examples that apply to what we are discussing in this chapter. "There is that speaketh like the piercings of a sword: but the tongue of the wise *is* health" (Proverbs 12:18). "The words of a man's mouth *are as* deep waters, *and* the wellspring of wisdom *as* a flowing brook" (Proverbs 18:4). Going through Proverbs to learn God's encouragement for words is a valuable study for a family as you undertake learning conversation skills.

IS CONVERSATION EDIFYING?

Remember this verse? "Let no corrupt communication proceed out of your mouth, but that which is good to the use of edifying, that it may minister grace unto the hearers" (Ephesians 4:29). Essentially it tells us to put off bad words and put on good ones for the benefit of the listener. In helping our children learn conversation skills, we need to give them some useful guidelines with which to evaluate the words of their conversations. A simple standard would be that they use edifying words.

Most of us enjoy eating because food tastes good, and it gives us energy. It is the same with an edifying conversation. It is enjoyable, and it builds up. "Let us therefore follow after the things which make for peace, and things wherewith one may edify another" (Romans 14:19).

According to *Strong's Talking Greek and Hebrew Dictionary*, the Greek word for edify means "to build." To have an edifying conversation, we discuss something that has value and will enrich or build up in some way. For Christians, the primary type of an edifying conversation is one that builds up spiritually.

"Good morning, Mom," Ryan greets Mom as he walks into the dining room for breakfast. "I am very hungry, and breakfast smells great. I am excited to tell you about what I read in my Bible this morning."

"Good morning, Ryan. I sure love you. Tell me what you are excited about."

"I was reading in 1 Corinthians 10 today, and I was very convicted. It was talking about the Israelites murmuring in the desert, and then some of them were destroyed. Then it said that was an example for us. That made me think about murmuring and how easy it is for me to be a murmurer. I realized that not only does God not like murmuring, but I don't think you or Dad or anyone else in our family likes it either. I really want to stop murmuring."

"You know, Ryan, that is convicting to me too. I was standing here murmuring in my heart about my frustration over the toaster not working very well. I think the Lord would rather have me thank Him for our breakfast and the tools He has provided to help me prepare it," Mom responds.

When our children were younger, we had them pick one verse each day from their individual morning Bible reading to copy into a notebook. It was to be a verse of personal application to their lives, and then they were to journal a few sentences about why they picked that verse. If you do that with your children, it will help them progress from simply reading words of Scripture to applying it to something that is real in their lives. It will enable them more easily and quickly to be able to edify others by telling them what they read that day and using the verse in appropriate situations.

Obviously, edifying conversation will be a growing process for our children under our tutelage. An eight-year-old will struggle with having edifying words. However, by the time he is thirteen, he should be well on his way to success in that area of his conversation.

WHAT IS THE CRITERIA OF PHILIPPIANS 4:8?

We could look at Philippians 4:8 to give us some aspects to define edifying conversation as we teach our children. "Finally, brethren, whatsoever things are true, whatsoever things *are* honest, whatsoever things *are* just, whatsoever things *are* pure, whatsoever things *are* lovely, whatsoever things *are* of good report; if *there be* any virtue, and if *there be* any praise, think on these things" (Philippians 4:8).

If we think about these things, they become the basis for our conversations. The same would hold true for our children. It starts with the heart and works out through the words. "But those things which proceed out of the mouth come forth from the heart..." (Matthew 15:18).

Our children's words are to be true, honest, and just. For many children, honesty is a battle that they will wage against their flesh with the help of their parents. "Lying lips *are* abomination to the LORD: but they that deal truly *are* his delight" (Proverbs 12:22). "Wherefore putting away lying, speak every man truth with his neighbour: for we are members one of another" (Ephesians 4:25).

When teaching honesty in conversation, we will also be teaching them appropriateness. "Whoso keepeth his mouth and his tongue keepeth his soul from troubles" (Proverbs 21:23).

What parent hasn't had a child loudly ask an honest question in the supermarket: "Why is that man so fat?" The child speaks truth, but he hasn't learned that it isn't appropriate to say someone is fat. The motive of love along with our instruction will help our children learn to align truth with appropriateness. "The lips of the righteous know what is acceptable: but the mouth of the wicked *speaketh* frowardness" (Proverbs 10:32).

Next we find that words are to be pure and lovely. That means our children are to be gracious and pleasant in their conversations. "The words of a wise man's mouth *are* gracious; but the lips of a fool will swallow up himself" (Ecclesiastes 10:12).

Compare these two conversations.

"Jason and Jennifer, I thought you might enjoy playing a game while your mother and I talk."

"Okay."

On the other hand, this could have been the response:

"Thank you for the game you got out for us to play."

As parents we will be involved in the process of directing our children toward pure and lovely words. We will instruct them, but as time progresses and we see failures, we will correct those failures.

"Hear, ye children, the instruction of a father, and attend to know understanding" (Proverbs 4:1).

Pure, lovely words will be the kinds of words mentioned in 1 Corinthians 13. These words will be winsome and upright words that will allow our children to exhort others down the right path when that might be needed. "And I myself also am persuaded of you, my brethren, that ye also are full of goodness, filled with all knowledge, able also to admonish one another" (Romans 15:14).

"The thoughts of the wicked *are* an abomination to the Lord: but *the words* of the pure *are* pleasant words" (Proverbs 15:26). Here is another word that describes conversation that comes from a pure heart—pleasant. What a delightful connotation "pleasant" holds! Let's encourage our children to use pleasant words.

WILL YOUR CHILDREN HAVE GOOD REPORTS?

Lastly, Philippians 4 says our words should be filled with good reports, virtue, and praise. "*As* cold waters to a thirsty soul, so *is* good news from a far country" (Proverbs 25:25). Good reports will eliminate tattling, a problem common among siblings. "A talebearer revealeth secrets: but he that is of a faithful spirit concealeth the matter" (Proverbs 11:13).

Here is another verse that shows us the importance of helping our children toward good reports rather than tattling: "Where no wood is, *there* the fire goeth out: so where *there is* no talebearer, the strife ceaseth" (Proverbs 26:20). Good reports stop our children from speaking negative or critical words. With a good report, virtue, and praise comes the encouragement of another.

Jimmy runs to Mommy and reports, "Sandra is playing with the guinea pigs. She's not doing her chores."

Think about how much better this conversation would be.

"Sandra, I know Mommy wants you to finish your chores before you play with the guinea pigs. My chores are done. I will help you with yours." After Jimmy and Sandra complete her chores, Jimmy runs to Mommy and reports, "Sandra finished her chores. Now she is playing with the guinea pigs."

Of course, there may be times when one child should let you know what a sibling is doing or isn't doing, particularly when sin is involved. However, even in that process, a child can learn to have a humble spirit that is more concerned for his sibling spiritually than he is for getting that sibling in trouble. In this case, even though it isn't positive news that he is telling, it is actually a good report because the information is shared only with the parent and will be for the benefit of the sibling.

CAN EDIFICATION COME THROUGH GRATITUDE?

"In every thing give thanks: for this is the will of God in Christ Jesus concerning you" (1 Thessalonians 5:18). Gratitude is almost always appropriate and edifying in a conversation. Our children confess Jesus Christ when they express gratitude to Him for what He has done for them and His blessings in their lives in conversations. "O give thanks unto the LORD; call upon his name: make known his deeds among the people" (Psalms 105:1).

Thanking others for what they have done causes them to feel loved and appreciated. "I thank my God upon every remembrance of you" (Philippians 1:3). These are all things we want our children to learn.

Contrast these two scenarios. Breakfast finishes. Bobby dashes to put his dishes in the dishwasher and then races for his bedroom. In this case, there is no gratitude expressed for breakfast, no edification happening.

Now let's try this again. Breakfast has just finished. Bobby clears his dishes. "Thank you, Mommy, for breakfast. I was hungry, and I really liked it. I know it takes you a while to make. Thank you for my delicious breakfast." A grateful heart will have this kind of response, and those words of gratitude build Mommy up. That is powerful—a little boy who can edify his mother through simple words of thankfulness.

It should be easy for our children to be grateful if we have modeled that for them. It is important that we are expressing appreciation for anything they do for us and also for what others do for us.

ARE YOUR CHILDREN USING GOOD WORDS?

Teri remembers a saying her parents often spoke to her while she was growing up: "If you can't say something nice, don't say anything at all." Perhaps that sums up the good words the Lord desires in conversation. Good words in our children's conversations are fueled by hearts that love others. Learning to set a self-focus aside to put one's attention on another is a positive step in a child's spiritual maturity. It will be manifested in his conversations.

In addition, his life must be conforming to the direction Scripture has for us. "Even a child is known by his doings, whether his work *be* pure, and whether *it be* right" (Proverbs 20:11). The Lord expects children to first learn and then do what is right and in line with what the Word teaches.

Our children enhance the usefulness of their conversations if they use the Word freely and frequently as they talk. We are told in Ephesians 4:29 that words should be edifying. Philippians 4:8 gives a guide to help us define for our children what exactly would be edifying. As they learn to speak words that are honest, pure, and of good report, they will edify their listeners. "A man hath joy by the answer of his mouth: and a word *spoken* in due season, how good *is it*" (Proverbs 15:23)! Think about the blessing your children will be throughout their lives if they are grateful encouragers who love to give a good report. We believe God will use our children for His glory as they develop God-honoring conversation skills.

THE PRACTICAL SIDE

IN REAL LIFE

We encourage our children to have edifying conversations at church and always. Often we discuss edifying questions we can ask other members of the church. We might ask the following questions:

"What chapter are you reading in the Bible?"

"What has God been teaching you lately?"

"What Scripture are you memorizing?"

"What is your favorite hymn?"

Our children then will share their answers to the question with the person they are talking to. We encourage the children not only to ask these questions to those who are the same age, but also to younger children, older children, or parents. Sometimes I will give the children "challenge" questions to ask one of the adults. For example:

"Would you tell me about your salvation experience?"

"How do you spend your devotional time?"

We share our conversations with each other later while eating a special treat!

BOILING IT DOWN

Teach your children:

- The motive and foundation for good conversation needs to be love. "Charity suffereth long, *and* is kind; charity envieth not; charity vaunteth not itself, is not puffed up, Doth not behave itself unseemly, seeketh not her own, is not easily provoked, thinketh no evil; Rejoiceth not in iniquity, but rejoiceth in the truth; Beareth all things, believeth all things, hopeth all things, endureth all things" (1 Corinthians 13:4-7).

- Obedience to God's Word produces powerful conversations.

- They need to have pure hearts in order to not be conversation hypocrites. "A good man out of the good treasure of his heart bringeth forth that which is good; and an evil man out of the evil treasure of his heart bringeth forth that which is evil: for of the abundance of the heart his mouth speaketh" (Luke 6:45).

- They should regularly speak of Christ through conversations. "That if thou shalt confess with thy mouth the Lord Jesus, and shalt believe in thine heart that God hath raised him from the dead, thou shalt be saved. For with the heart man believeth unto righteousness; and with the mouth confession is made unto salvation" (Romans 10:9-10).

- The Word of God has power, authority, and persuasiveness when used in conversations. "Speaking to yourselves in psalms and hymns and spiritual songs, singing and making melody in your heart to the Lord" (Ephesians 5:19). "Let the word of Christ dwell in you richly in all wisdom; teaching and admonishing one another in psalms and hymns and spiritual songs, singing with grace in your hearts to the Lord" (Colossians 3:16).

- They should put off bad words and put on good ones for the benefit of the listener.

- Their words should be edifying. "Let no corrupt communication proceed out of your mouth, but that which is good to the use of edifying, that it may minister grace unto the hearers" (Ephesians 4:29).

- Gratitude is almost always appropriate in a conversation. "If you can't say something nice, don't say anything at all."

MAKING IT STICK

Remember to take notes on each assignment, practice, or evaluation.

1. Rate yourself (1-10) concerning your use of the Word in conversation. Then rate your children.
2. Rate yourself (1-10) concerning your conversation using the following criteria. Then rate your children.

   Are the words:

   - Loving?
   - Edifying?
3. Read aloud the conversations in this chapter and discuss them with your family.

CHAPTER 5

ARE THERE CONVERSATION DANGERS AND CAUTIONS?

Each of us is accountable to the Lord for our words, and they are powerful. "Death and life *are* in the power of the tongue: and they that love it shall eat the fruit thereof" (Proverbs 18:21). Just as there are laws in our country governing how we drive in order to save lives, God gives us directions concerning our words since they also can have life-and-death consequences.

Our children need to learn that their words are important to God, and that He has direction for them concerning their words. We as parents are the vehicles to lead our children to that understanding and application.

SHOULD WE ELIMINATE IDLE WORDS?

"But I say unto you, That every idle word that men shall speak, they shall give account thereof in the day of judgment" (Matthew 12:36). *Strong's Greek and Hebrew Dictionary* defines "idle" as useless. Jesus is telling us that we are going to be held accountable for every useless word. If we are going to answer for even useless words, we can be sure we are accountable for every bad or wicked word as well. The Lord hears every single word we speak. Our children should know that He wants their conversations to be like the ones we discussed in the last chapter—edifying and filled with truth, thanksgiving, praise, graciousness, and good reports.

SHOULD WE ELIMINATE FOOLISH TALK?

"But fornication, and all uncleanness, or covetousness, let it not be once named among you, as becometh saints; Neither filthiness, nor foolish talking, nor jesting, which are not convenient: but rather giving of thanks" (Ephesians 5:3-4). Two types of idle words are foolish talking and jesting. Children are particularly notorious for these types of conversations, but adults can be guilty as well. Look at all the evil we are admonished away from in these verses along with foolish talking and jesting. That should tell us that foolish talking and jesting are much more serious to the Lord than they usually are in our minds.

Children tend toward foolishness, and that will then come out in their conversations. "Foolishness *is* bound in the heart of a child..." (Proverbs 22:15). As parents, we should teach our children what is foolish talk and direct them away from it. Too often parents excuse foolish talking because they are children. The reality, though, is that during these years our children are in our home, we want to be teaching them right conversation versus wrong conversation. If we let the foolish talking go, it will be perpetuated into adulthood. All one has to do is listen to a group of average young men talking to each other to know the truth of that.

In our family, we still occasionally talk about the foolishness of our children's Grandpa and Benny stories. They went through a phase of making up stories and recording them. The theme was a fictional Grandpa and Benny. The stories were totally folly and foolishness. We didn't know enough in our parenting at that point to eliminate the foolishness and direct our children to edification. Those stories have provided us a good example of foolish talking in children.

IS JOKING BENEFICIAL?

Jesting or joking is very accepted among Christians. It is even prevalent from the pulpit during sermons. For example, I (Steve) recall from many years ago a Sunday morning service. The pastor spoke into the microphone and said to the worship leader, "I'm so grateful for you, brother. You are one bright guy." Everyone was pleased with the word of appreciation from the pastor for his worship leader. Then the pastor went on to say, "That bald head of yours causes such a reflection, I can hardly see past you." Most laughed, and then waited for the worship leader to say something cutting back to the pastor. In my heart, though, I knew those words stung deep into the worship leader because he was young and quite self-conscious about his bare head.

What does Scripture say about joking? "As a mad *man* who casteth firebrands, arrows, and death, So *is* the man *that* deceiveth his neighbour, and saith, Am not I in sport?" (Proverbs 26:18-19). Scripture tells us that if we find ourselves saying "only joking" we are actually deceiving the one to whom we are saying it. It also indicates that those words come from someone who will end up destroying a relationship, not building it up.

How often do you hear the words in your home, "I was only joking"? Maybe you have been the model for a joking mentality in your home. Consider how often another family member is at the root of the joking. The one joking, and perhaps the rest of the family, is greatly enjoying the joke, but the recipient might not be. It is possible a child needs to be corrected and the jesting is part of that correction. However, evaluating this verse, it would seem that the correction would be better administered directly rather than in the roundabout way of joking that often causes the recipient to feel belittled.

Let us give you an example.

As Sally gets into the van on Sunday morning, Dad says, "Here she comes. Miss Sally Slowpoke—always the last one out."

Sally looks unhappy and begins to defend herself. "James was in the bathroom so I had to wait a long time for him, and then I needed to get my Bible. I hurried as fast as I could."

"Oh, Sally, don't be so defensive. I was only joking!" Dad responds.

This kind of joking might also be called sarcasm. If there is a portion of truth in what was said, think about the difference had Dad simply waited to give his instruction without jesting during his one-on-one meeting with Sally that week. He could have brought up her tendency to be the last one out and helped her figure out methods to be more prepared for departing on time. He would have helped and equipped her, not caused her to feel put down, and he would have avoided the biblical injunction against jesting.

If the joke isn't true, then obviously it is a lie. God hates lying. "Lying lips *are* abomination to the LORD: but they that deal truly *are* his delight" (Proverbs 12:22). When we end with, "I was only joking," in essence we are saying, "I was lying." Let's teach our children not to joke but to always be truthful, becoming a delight to God rather than an abomination. Look at the blessing that one simple instruction in conversation can be to our children.

"Excellent speech becometh not a fool: much less do lying lips a prince" (Proverbs 17:7). This verse talks both of foolishness and lying. The fool's speech will not be excellent, and lying doesn't become a child of a king.

If you stop joking, does that mean your home becomes solemn and gloomy? Absolutely not. Ephesians 5 tells us the words that are to replace joking. They are words of thanksgiving. Those are the words that will bring joy, delight, and contentment to your family.

CAN FEWER WORDS BE BETTER?

We have already discussed the person who talks on and on, either about herself like Mrs. Monroe or about endless stories. While the person speaking is greatly enjoying the conversation, the listeners are generally bored. "Surely the serpent will bite without enchantment; and a babbler is no better" (Ecclesiastes 10:11). This verse gives us a negative picture of the person who is an incessant talker—a babbler.

We want our children to understand that conversation is give and take, back and forth, with a motive of love.

"In the multitude of words there wanteth not sin: but he that refraineth his lips *is* wise" (Proverbs 10:19). This verse isn't telling our children not to talk, but it is warning them of the possibility of sinning if they do not control their words. It is pretty easy for any one to find himself involved in gossip, tale bearing, or even speaking hurtful words when angry or disappointed.

"Even a fool, when he holdeth his peace, is counted wise: *and* he that shutteth his lips *is esteemed* a man of understanding" (Proverbs 17:28). There are times for children to learn to be quiet. We have observed the propensity of our children to speak as if they are authorities on a subject about which they have no real experience or knowledge. Those conversations are the ones our children should listen to and ask questions about rather than giving answers.

WHAT ARE SOME WRONG WORDS?

Scripture gives us many kinds of wrong words that we can teach our children to avoid and explain why they are not to be part of our conversations. Simply by helping them learn right words for conversations, they will naturally avoid the wrong ones. However, these verses and examples should cement in their minds the importance of using good words.

"The words of his mouth *are* iniquity and deceit: he hath left off to be wise, *and* to do good" (Psalms 36:3). This verse is telling about the wicked. Children can struggle with being deceitful. They should be instructed in the importance of truthful words and avoiding deceit.

Flattery, which is insincere praise, is something our children are to avoid. Flattery seems to be focused on the person speaking wanting to gain something for himself. He has a selfish motive. Praise, on the other hand, desires only to build the recipient up.

"For neither at any time used we flattering words, as ye know, nor a cloke of covetousness; God *is* witness" (1 Thessalonians 2:5). Flattery is soundly condemned in Scripture. In the following verse we see that a rebuke is actually better in a relationship than flattery. "He that rebuketh a man afterwards shall find more favour than he that flattereth with the tongue" (Proverbs 28:23).

"A lying tongue hateth *those that are* afflicted by it; and a flattering mouth worketh ruin" (Proverbs 26:28). Earlier we discussed the importance of our children's words being truthful. Here we observe the flattering mouth associated with lying and having a negative outcome of its own. We don't want ruin for our children, so they need to see flattery in the same category as evil words and know that they are words to completely avoid.

"A man that flattereth his neighbour spreadeth a net for his feet" (Proverbs 29:5). Here we discover that flattery sets a trap for the one who is using the flattery. The outcome will likely be negative.

Help your children learn to give honest praise without flattery. That can be hard for an adult, let alone a child. As specific situations arise, we think you will find teachable moments to help you define and explain to your children the differences between flattery and praise.

For example, John notices that Anna is playing with his favorite toy. He walks over to her and says, "Anna, I love how you play with your doll Jennifer. You look like the perfect, happy mommy when you are holding your dolly."

"Really?" Anna replies as she puts down the toy to go find her Jennifer doll.

Obviously, John was not sincere in his compliment of his sister. It was flattery. He had an agenda and figured out a way to accomplish his goal. How much better it would have been for John to ask Anna directly for permission to play with the toy and to pay his compliment another time, when Anna was playing with her doll. Then it would have been sincere praise.

We will want to direct our children away from evil and wicked talk. "To deliver thee from the way of the evil *man*, from the man that speaketh froward things" (Proverbs 2:12). It is possible that children growing up in a Christian home may not know what is evil and wicked. We recently heard of a Christian young man who said if he is around worldly people and hears a word he is not familiar with, he assumes it is one he doesn't want to repeat.

Even though Teri did not come to know the Lord Jesus as Savior until her early twenties, she remembers a conversation with her dad about wrong words. One afternoon when she was about thirteen, she came home from being with her friends and repeated to her father something that had been said to her. Even though Teri's dad was an army officer and had been around plenty of bad language, he was shocked by what his sweet daughter had just said. He soundly told her that no young lady used that word, and he never wanted to hear her say it again. That is a conversation that had quite an impact on Teri!

ARE WE RESPONSIBLE FOR HURTFUL WORDS?

Are you familiar with the saying that goes like this: "Sticks and stones may break my bones, but words can never hurt me"? In reality, though, the emotional pain some words cause can be much more damaging than the physical pain of an injury. Remember the words of the pastor to the worship leader earlier? Even though spoken in a good natured way, they still hurt the worship leader.

"Who whet their tongue like a sword, *and* bend *their bows to shoot* their arrows, *even* bitter words" (Psalms 64:3).

"They have sharpened their tongues like a serpent; adders' poison *is* under their lips" (Psalms 140:3).

"The words of a talebearer *are* as wounds, and they go down into the innermost parts of the belly" (Proverbs 18:8).

As we teach our children about conversation, we help them avoid words that are like swords, arrows, wounds, and poison. Sometimes children do not have an awareness of how others might receive their words so part of our job will be to direct them toward that understanding.

SHOULD WE BE CAUTIOUS OF OTHERS' WORDS?

We also want to educate our children by providing biblical cautions regarding the words others will speak to them. There are times when it is not appropriate for them to remain in the conversation. Recently Teri was talking to a woman who told her that she had just read the history concerning a wicked profession. Teri did not want the conversation to continue so she quickly changed the subject.

"The heart of the righteous studieth to answer: but the mouth of the wicked poureth out evil things" (Proverbs 15:28).

Our children must learn what is truthful according to Scripture through the study of God's Word in their personal Bible time and through family Bible time so they are not a target for wicked influence.

"And be not conformed to this world: but be ye transformed by the renewing of your mind, that ye may prove what *is* that good, and acceptable, and perfect, will of God" (Romans 12:2).

"The simple believeth every word: but the prudent *man* looketh well to his going" (Proverbs 14:15).

"Let no man deceive you with vain words: for because of these things cometh the wrath of God upon the children of disobedience" (Ephesians 5:6).

When our children are grounded in the Word, they are not as susceptible to the deception of the world, its philosophies, and it pleasures. You can have some great conversations with your children at home discussing those things you hear or see as a family that are deceptive and contrary to God's Word. By doing this, you will cement in your children's minds the truth of Scripture and demonstrate for them the logic involved in contradicting Satan's deceptive, but enticing, words.

For example, for many years Steve took the boys to City Union Mission once a month to minister. Those Saturday mission services gave Steve perfect opportunities to discuss what Scripture says about alcohol and drug use, the physical dangers of it, and the destruction it does to families. The children were able to observe firsthand the points Steve would make in his conversations with them.

What about modesty? Do you want to teach your children to dress modestly and to avoid looking at immodesty? Being in public where there is much immodesty affords the opportunity to discuss modesty with our children. We can tell them why we have modesty standards and why we don't want to dress as the world dresses. These conversations come up naturally as we are exposed to the ungodliness of the world.

HOW ARE OUR CHILDREN TO RESPOND TO HURTFUL WORDS?

There will be times our children hear words spoken to them that are swords, arrows, wounds, or poison. God's Word tells us to ignore those words. "Also take no heed unto all words that are spoken; lest thou hear thy servant curse thee" (Ecclesiastes 7:21). There will be a biblical path toward ignoring the hurtful words, such as praying, forgiving, and putting the truth of the Word into our children's minds.

"Be careful for nothing; but in every thing by prayer and supplication with thanksgiving let your requests be made known unto God. And the peace of God, which passeth all understanding, shall keep your hearts and minds through Christ Jesus" (Philippians 4:6-7).

"Forbearing one another, and forgiving one another . . ." (Colossians 3:13).

"Casting down imaginations, and every high thing that exalteth itself against the knowledge of God, and bringing into captivity every thought to the obedience of Christ" (2 Corinthians 10:5).

We know of a young man who goes to public school and rides on the school bus. He has chosen to read his Bible on the ride and as a result receives unkind and mocking comments from the other children. His mother has encouraged him through verses such as:

"Blessed are ye, when *men* shall revile you, and persecute *you*, and shall say all manner of evil against you falsely, for my sake. Rejoice, and be exceeding glad: for great *is* your reward in heaven: for so persecuted they the prophets which were before you" (Matthew 5:11-12).

WORDS—FRIEND OR FOE?

While words are powerful allies for our children in relationship building and success in life, the opposite is true as well. They can just as quickly tear apart a relationship or yank our children into an abyss of problems.

Helping our children see that they are accountable to God for their words gives them a higher standard and authority than simply pleasing their parents. As they learn words to avoid in their conversations, they receive God's protection on their lives. When they evaluate their words against a Scriptural standard and eliminate the wrong ones, their hearts grow in wisdom. Because they love others, they don't bore by monopolizing a conversation, talking only of themselves and telling only their stories.

This process takes time, and it involves our investment in our children's lives. We will have to be aware of the conversations our children hear or are involved in, and then help them understand wrong words and conversations to be avoided. That means having more conversations with our children as we instruct them in the dangers inherent in words. We must be committed to the task of raising sons and daughters who are godly conversationalists.

THE PRACTICAL SIDE

IN REAL LIFE

Our family uses the last Sunday of every month to evangelize downtown. We are confronted with people who refuse our tracts or discussion in an evil way. For example, "If you give me that, I'll burn it." Someone else might say, "No way!" We respond by not saying anything and moving along. Our facial expressions are ones of love not anger.

BOILING IT DOWN

Teach your children:

- Each is accountable to the Lord for his words, and words are powerful. "Death and life *are* in the power of the tongue: and they that love it shall eat the fruit thereof" (Proverbs 18:21).
- Jesus wants conversations to be edifying and filled with truth, thanksgiving, praise, graciousness, and good reports, not idle, useless words.
- Two types of idle words are foolish talking and jesting.
- No joking, only truthfulness.

- Be cautious of too many words. "In the multitude of words there wanteth not sin: but he that refraineth his lips *is* wise" (Proverbs 10:19).

- Be careful not to speak as an authority. "Even a fool, when he holdeth his peace, is counted wise: *and* he that shutteth his lips *is esteemed* a man of understanding" (Proverbs 17:28).

- Do not be deceitful. "The words of his mouth *are* iniquity and deceit: he hath left off to be wise, *and* to do good" (Psalms 36:3).

- Give honest praise without flattery.

- Do not have evil or wicked words. "To deliver thee from the way of the evil *man*, from the man that speaketh froward things" (Proverbs 2:12).

- Avoid words that are like swords, arrows, wounds, and poison.

  "Who whet their tongue like a sword, *and* bend *their bows to shoot* their arrows, *even* bitter words" (Psalms 64:3).

  "They have sharpened their tongues like a serpent; adders' poison *is* under their lips" (Psalms 140:3).

  "The words of a talebearer *are* as wounds, and they go down into the innermost parts of the belly" (Proverbs 18:8).

- Don't listen to wicked conversation. "The heart of the righteous studieth to answer: but the mouth of the wicked poureth out evil things" (Proverbs 15:28).

- Learn what is truthful according to Scripture through the study of God's Word in personal Bible time and through family Bible time so as not to be a target for deception.

  > "And be not conformed to this world: but be ye transformed by the renewing of your mind, that ye may prove what *is* that good, and acceptable, and perfect, will of God" (Romans 12:2).
  >
  > "The simple believeth every word: but the prudent *man* looketh well to his going" (Proverbs 14:15).
  >
  > "Let no man deceive you with vain words: for because of these things cometh the wrath of God upon the children of disobedience" (Ephesians 5:6).

- Ignore hurtful words. "Also take no heed unto all words that are spoken; lest thou hear thy servant curse thee" (Ecclesiastes 7:21).

- Pray, forgive, and put the truth of the Word into the mind when faced with hurtful words.

  > "Be careful for nothing; but in every thing by prayer and supplication with thanksgiving let your requests be made known unto God.

> And the peace of God, which passeth all understanding, shall keep your hearts and minds through Christ Jesus" (Philippians 4:6-7).
>
> "Forbearing one another, and forgiving one another..." (Colossians 3:13).
>
> "Casting down imaginations, and every high thing that exalteth itself against the knowledge of God, and bringing into captivity every thought to the obedience of Christ" (2 Corinthians 10:5).

MAKING IT STICK

Remember to take notes on each assignment, practice, or evaluation.

1. Do you, your spouse, or any of your children talk too much?
2. Is anyone having trouble with the wrong words described in this chapter? If so, document in your notebook or on your computer who and which category.
    - Idle words
    - Foolish talk
    - Jesting
    - Deceitful words

- Flattering words
- Evil words
- Hurtful words

3. As a family, memorize verses that have to do with areas of wrong words that family members are struggling with.
4. At mealtime or other family discussions, have each person evaluate how he is doing in those areas listed above where you evaluated him. Record their personal evaluations. Encourage those who are not doing so well on how they can do better, and praise those doing well.
5. Read and discuss the conversations in this chapter.

CHAPTER 6

HOW DO I HELP MY CHILDREN IMPROVE?

The Dixbees are a typical Christian family. After praying for their evening meal, Dad says, "Tell us about your day, kids."

"It was fine," sixteen-year-old Morgan begins.

"Mine too," fourteen-year-old Hunter adds.

"What did you do?" Dad works toward getting more conversation from the children.

"Oh, not much," Hunter answers.

"Hmm, I don't know," Morgan says.

Dad gives up on the conversation with his children and focuses on finishing his dinner so he can get to his computer to answer some pressing e-mails.

Let's observe the Dixbees after they have worked on their conversational skills. Not only can they now talk to each other, but they enjoy lingering at the dinner table over their family conversations.

After praying for their meal, Dad says, "Tell us about your day, kids."

"It was a normal school day for me," Hunter responds. "I have been struggling with equations in my algebra. Mom has been encouraging me to pray and ask the Lord to help me. Today I finally felt like I was making some progress. It felt so good."

"You know, son, math was hard for me, too, but there was a great sense of accomplishment when I understood something. I didn't know the Lord when I was a teen so I didn't have His help like you do," Dad encourages. "What about you, Morgan?"

"School was fine, but what I was really excited about was starting to work on an apron I am making. I had washed and dried the fabric yesterday. Today I was able to cut the whole thing out so tomorrow afternoon I will be ready to begin sewing."

Then Hunter introduces another topic for discussion: "Dad and Mom, I'd like to tell you what the Lord has been teaching me through my Bible time in the morning. I'm reading in Jeremiah, and it is so convicting. I wonder if there aren't a lot of similarities between today and Bible-time Israel."

"Son," Dad responds. "I have felt the same thing as I read Jeremiah. Whenever I read that book, I come away so amazed at God's patience with Israel and then with the world today."

Morgan chimes in: "Dad, do you think God could be running out of patience with mankind?"

"He certainly would be justified if He is. It is amazing how little interest most people have in the Lord Jesus or anything that has to do with the Bible."

Hunter remarked, "In Jeremiah, I noticed how much Jeremiah pleads with the people to leave their sin and follow the Lord. He begs them to repent, but they seemed bent on continuing on the path they were on. They wanted to do what they wanted to do."

"Wow," Morgan says. "That does sound a lot like what is happening today."

Mom had been silent until now. "You are right, Morgan. It grieves my heart when I observe the things our nation is embracing that the Lord despises."

Dad continues, "I have always loved this verse because it tells it like it is. 'If my people, which are called by my name, shall humble themselves, and pray, and seek my face, and turn from their wicked ways; then will I hear from heaven, and will forgive their sin, and will heal their land.' That's 2 Chronicles 7:14, and it says that we are to humble ourselves, pray, seek God, and turn from our wicked ways. It is very important that we examine our lives first to make sure that is what we have done. As long as Christians embrace the wickedness of the world, we won't have healing in our land."

The discussion easily continues and moves on to other subjects until it is time for dinner cleanup and family Bible time.

CAN CONVERSATION SKILLS BE TAUGHT?

Did you feel badly for Dad as you observed him trying to draw his family together through personal communication in that first conversation at the dinner table? Did you appreciate the depth of conversation that was taking place amongst the family members after they had learned and practiced good conversation skills?

Conversation is something that can be taught to our children. They can become good conversationalists—starting in our homes and working from there to others with whom they come in contact. You are beginning to do just that as you go through the "Boiling It Down" and "Making It Stick" sections of this book with your children.

As you are involved in this process of teaching your children conversation skills, get the children's buy-in to the learning process. When you read them the conversation examples, ask them who they want to be like—the first example or the second? Challenge them with the goal of learning, practice, and growth. "The heart of the wise teacheth his mouth, and addeth learning to his lips" (Proverbs 16:23).

The family is God's training ground for many basic aspects of life. With conversation, that means that we first concentrate on teaching and practicing within the family.

DOES REMOVING DISTRACTIONS HELP CONVERSATION?

If we want to be successful teaching conversation skills, we need to eliminate hindrances to conversation. In our modern era, there are many activities that draw our attention or hold our focus, and they interfere with the ability to talk as a family. Anything that we give our attention to above the person who is talking is a distraction.

For example, watching television or movies is a common pastime. It takes a great amount of time, and it doesn't allow for conversation. As a matter of fact, if anyone tries to start a conversation in the middle of a good show or a movie, those intent on what they are watching will tell the person who is talking to be quiet so nothing is missed.

Video games also draw the attention away from verbal interactions because of the need for intense concentration and a desire not to be interrupted. Video games, along with TV and movies, tend to turn our children's minds off of productive thinking and onto the entertainment mentality. Perhaps the reason many children have so much trouble conversing is because they don't have many original thoughts. Their minds are filled with whatever they are watching or playing. We encourage families to institute a no television and no video game policy.

Other things that can be distractions to conversation include cell phones, iPads, computers, and even books. You can probably think of some that are specific to your family. These distractions are not ones that need to be completely eliminated but rather managed and controlled. That means we first model and then teach our children that when someone tries to converse with us when we are involved with doing something else, we make the relationship a priority above the task. We turn our face and our focus from the task to the person who is talking to us.

In our family, Teri's computer desk faces out the window. That means when someone comes into the room, her back is to them. She has made it a practice to turn away from her computer to face and look at the person who has entered the room wanting to talk to her. That completely eliminates the computer as a distraction. If there is a reason she needs to quickly finish what she is doing before she can turn her attention, she will say, "Just a moment. I am almost done."

A final distraction from conversation is simply being too busy. When the family is involved in various activities, their ability to talk is hampered because their time is filled with those activities. If parents are the busy ones, their minds are engaged in what is keeping them busy, and they aren't available for conversing with their children.

WHAT ARE TALK-FRIENDLY TIMES?

As parents, we can provide an incentive to talk by opening up talk-friendly times in our schedules. We gain the added benefit of building not only conversation skills but also vital relationships.

Probably the most convenient family conversation time is at meals. However, if the family is seldom together at meal time, the purpose of learning conversation is defeated. That means working your schedule so that you have plenty of meals together, and then focusing on conversation skills throughout the meal. This is ideal because everyone is together and can benefit from the practice their turn affords while observing others practice.

In addition, two wonderful talking times are before and after family Bible time. Our family talks throughout dinner, and we can still sit for an hour in the living room before family Bible time for more enjoyable conversation. We are relaxed, without even the small distractions of serving and passing food that occurs at the dinner table.

Putting children to bed at night affords another opportunity for conversation with your children. It could be the time for a one-on-one conversation with a particular child, or it might be a smaller group conversation with the one-gender siblings sharing a bedroom. We have found when one of us lies down on a bed next to a child, conversation quickly opens and progresses.

Consider the possibilities of conversation learning and practice in your vehicle when running errands or going to an activity with one or more family members. Frequently we will find ourselves with just one child in the car with us, and then we can evaluate that child's conversation skills. We will also be able to work individually with the child without others being involved. If there are several together on the outing, it is still great conversation time with the group.

Going for a walk is another opportunity for working with your children on their conversation skills. Engage the children walking with you in conversation and encourage them to practice what they have been learning.

One family shared another talk-friendly time. This past winter they spent several nights shelling pecans together around the kitchen table. The children and parents all talked the entire time. It turned out to be a real blessing. For the Maxwells, we regularly need to put together ChorePacks—a simple chore tool for children that we assemble as a family and sell as part of the *Managers of Their*

Chores book. We all sit in the living room and talk while we spend about a half hour per evening working until the job is completed. What family projects do you have that you could accomplish while practicing conversation skills?

DO YOU KNOW THE ULTIMATE TALK-FRIENDLY TIME?

For over twenty years I (Steve) have had weekly one-on-one meetings with my children. When a child is about four or five, he begins having a meeting with me. It has been a rich time of heart sharing to which we all look forward each week. I would recommend that every dad begin the same practice. It is the perfect opportunity to develop conversational skills, in addition to the blessing of gaining a deeper relationship with your child.

For a weekly meeting, you will want to find a time that is consistent. It helps to schedule a time and place. We have ours after church while lunch is being prepared, and then after we eat lunch since I can't get through all the meetings before lunch.

The meeting place should be private and quiet. We generally have ours in the master bedroom. I sit in a glider chair, and the child flops on our bed. If it is cold, we sit in the basement by the wood stove. If the weather is nice, we go to the gliders on the front porch. One dad recently shared this about his meetings: "Venues that work well for us are a walk or a lunch date."

Make weekly individual meetings a priority for your time with your family. This will ensure that they will happen, and as a result, we believe they will deepen your ability to converse with each child.

HOW DO YOU INSTRUCT YOUR CHILDREN IN CONVERSATION?

Making conversation-skill learning purposeful means that you will instruct children using the background conversation information that you have already read in this book. We are helping you toward this goal with the "Boiling It Down" section in each chapter. You will want to pair that instruction with your own experience and what you personally think are important conversation skills.

Remember, as you assist your children in becoming conversationalists, that it is done gently. You want to lead and guide, without harshness or a critical spirit. "... and the sheep follow him: for they know his voice" (John 10:4). Jesus, the Good Shepherd, led the sheep, and we must gently lead our flock as well.

You started by defining conversations for your children. Regularly give some examples of bad conversations and good ones like we have done throughout this book. Your children can evaluate those conversations and tell you what was bad and what was good. Even without much instruction, they can probably figure out quite a bit just by listening to both kinds of conversations.

When you are going to be with others, encourage the children to listen carefully to the conversations around them. Then have a family discussion afterward to see what can be learned from them. When children hear good conversations, they can incorporate the positive conversation qualities in their own conversations. If there are negative aspects of the discussions, that can also be evaluated.

Regularly remind your children of why conversations are important. The children will see that part of your motive for a conversation emphasis is to build better, stronger, and more loving family relationships. That should be appealing to them. You can also draw them to the benefits conversation skills will bring to them in their adult lives, and how they will enhance their ability to minister to others and serve the Lord Jesus.

On an ongoing basis, discuss the kinds of words they should use, why those words are pleasing to the Lord, and the words they want to avoid. Remember to model for your children the use of Scripture, Bible stories, and references to the Lord, and encourage them to do the same anytime they can. "I will speak of thy testimonies also before kings, and will not be ashamed" (Psalms 119:46).

HOW CAN ONE PRACTICE CONVERSATION?

As the children develop comfort with their conversation skills in the family, you will want to broaden their experience and practice. You could start by inviting an extended family member, who is a believer, over for dinner. That might mean Dad and Mom are less active in the conversations so the children have the opportunity to talk.

You can also invite another person or family from your church over for dinner. It is certainly a bit easier if it is just one person, such as a young, single adult or a widow or widower. That allows the conversation to focus on that particular person so that it doesn't have to be spread between a couple or a whole family.

As conversation experience grows, having a family from church over for dinner allows a greater degree of not only practice but also ministry. The girls can have conversations with the visiting daughters and mom while the boys engage the other family's sons and father.

The next rung on the experience ladder will be conversations with nonbelievers. When you invite them into your home, you will be cautious to oversee conversations between them and your children. They will not have a sensitivity to what a Christian would consider appropriate topics for children's ears. Parents can stop or forestall what they don't want their children to hear.

Anytime your family is out in public, there are conversation possibilities. It could be talking to the checkout person while at the store. Maybe it is the teller at the bank when you stop by to do some banking. What about when you are waiting in line to return or purchase an item and there are people in front of you and behind? When you are out, be watchful for people with whom your children could begin a conversation, and help them initiate the conversation.

Church is another place for your children to practice conversation and minister through it. It is common for us to get into a rut of talking with a select group of people at church. Challenge your children to meet new people at church and to talk to those they don't know so well.

In the "Making It Stick" sections of this book, we encourage you with specific practical assignments. These are concrete and achievable. We believe they will be an asset to you as you help your children practice conversation skills.

HOW DO YOU ENHANCE LEARNING CONVERSATION?

Especially during the teaching phase of conversation skills, you will want to have frequent after-action discussions. Ask the family to evaluate the conversations, with you as parents giving input as well.

Then you can reinforce what the children did well and point out what could be improved upon. Be inspirational in these discussions, not discouraging. Major on the positive, and minor on the negative.

Role-play with the children how the conversations could have gone that would have made them better conversations. Then try to give them another chance to practice before too much time passes, while it is still fresh in their minds.

As you are teaching conversation skills, don't set your expectations too high. First recall that there will be age-appropriate conversation goals. We know that a five-year-old's conversation will not be like a ten-year-old's, and that a ten-year-old's will not be like his eighteen-year-old brother's. In addition, it is a learning process, and we are working with children. Remember the truth found in James 3:8: "But the tongue can no man tame; *it is* an unruly evil, full of deadly poison." They will regularly fail, learn from those failures, and then be able to try again.

You can expect there to be more bad conversations than good ones in the beginning. As a matter of fact, as you start you may have trouble getting your child to say anything, let alone have a meaningful conversation. That's okay. Work from there. Encourage your children and facilitate them in their conversations.

WILL WE PRACTICE CONVERSATION?

"Practice makes perfect" is a familiar saying to most of us, and it is as true for learning to be a good conversationalist as it is for other areas of our lives. You will be teaching your children the basics of conversations, but they have to have real-time, real-life conversations in order to hone their conversation skills.

Dad and Mom would be advised to privately discuss when, where, with whom, and with what supervision the children's newfound skills may be practiced. The children's age, family vision, and environment will all be factors to be considered. Then share with the children the "ground rules" for conversation development.

Practice in your home and other places when it is just your family, such as when you are driving somewhere. Then graduate to practice sessions when you invite others into your home, and finally take advantage of conversation opportunities when out in public.

After each conversation, evaluate what went well with the conversation and what didn't. You can offer practical suggestions for your children for the next time they get to test out their conversation skills. Then work to afford them another chance as quickly as possible.

If we will put the time and effort into teaching and practicing conversation skills, our children will learn them and also improve the skills they already have. To become skilled at anything, we can expect the need to practice, and good conversation skills are no exception.

We think that as you embark on this conversation-skills learning journey, you will be excited and encouraged by the quick progress your children will make. Their conversation skills will soon set your children head and shoulders above their peers, build their relationships with others, cause them to gain a hearing with those they come in contact with, and be a wonderful testimony for their Lord Jesus Christ.

THE PRACTICAL SIDE

IN REAL LIFE

The other day, while visiting the nursing home, we noticed our friend Ms. Leona was looking sad and depressed while sitting in her wheelchair. When thirteen-year-old Libby and I went to talk with her, Ms. Leona held Libby's hand while saying how much Libby reminded her of her own daughter many years ago. Ms. Leona is legally blind, so you have to get very close for her to be able to recognize your face. The next thing we knew, Ms. Leona started weeping while still holding Libby's hand. After finding out that Ms. Leona's daughter had recently passed away, we were able to comfort her, minister to her, and offer words of Scripture to encourage her. Ms. Leona continued to speak of her grief, all the while mentioning what her own "upcoming" funeral would be like and where it would be held. She was, at that moment, overcome with feelings of despair and death.

Because of our many visits to the nursing home and Libby's frequent conversations with Ms. Leona, as well as with many of the other residents there, Libby didn't feel uncomfortable holding Ms. Leona's hand or offering comfort to her. Those many occasions when they'd had regular conversations in the past allowed a ninety-year-old woman in a wheelchair and a thirteen-year-old girl to be able to communicate with just a comforting hand and a smile. The conversation ended with Ms. Leona looking forward to our next visit and even returning our smiles. Never underestimate the foundation for the future that a meaningful conversation can lay. The person that you offer an attentive ear to today may be the same person who is willing to listen to you tell them about Jesus tomorrow, in their time of need.

BOILING IT DOWN

Teach your children:

- That they can learn to be good conversationalists.
- That they need to learn, practice, and grow in their conversation skills. "The heart of the wise teacheth his mouth, and addeth learning to his lips" (Proverbs 16:23).
- Not to let distractions such as TV, movies, video games, cell phones, iPads, computers, or books keep them from conversations.
- That there are talk-friendly times, and they should work at talking to those around them.
- To receive your conversation instruction.
- To listen to conversations of others so that they can learn from them—both the good ones and the bad ones.

- To be willing to practice their conversation skills.
- To critique their conversations and ask others to as well.

MAKING IT STICK

Remember to take notes on each assignment, practice, or evaluation.

1. Discuss as a family conversation distractions. Plan ways to eliminate them.
2. Figure out the best talk-friendly times for your family, and put them in the schedule.
3. At dinner or evening family Bible time, have everyone take turns reporting on their day. You may have to be careful and give a time limit for each if you have a large family. When we do this, we have to limit the first reporters because otherwise we often don't have time to get through the whole family. Evaluate each child as to whether he is giving enough detail for everyone to understand but not talking too much. Evaluate and document each child's conversation.
4. At dinner or evening family Bible time, have everyone take turns telling what they read during their personal Bible time. Evaluate and document each child's conversation.

5. For a variation of this idea, you might try other topics, such as Scripture recently read, animals, activities, memories, holidays, or any other general-interest topics you can think of.
6. One-on-one practice. Find those times when you can be with just one child, and focus on conversation with him. Let him lead in the conversation and practice what he has been learning.

CHAPTER 7

HOW DO WE WORK WITH BEGINNERS?

We think these next three chapters are the most exciting ones in this book because it is time for your children to hone their conversation skills. Up to this point, they have had some basic conversation practices within your family, but now it is time to dive into the meat of conversation skill development for all stages of conversationalists—beginner, intermediate, and advanced.

Conversation instruction will vary depending on the age of the child. The younger the child, the more time and practice it takes for him to acquire his targeted goals. In this chapter, we will look at conversation goals for beginners and how to work toward those goals. Even if your child is older, we suggest you still go through the beginner information. There may be aspects of conversation that your older children should learn—maybe you too!

HOW DO WE HELP BEGINNERS?

We might think of conversation beginners as being young children, but it is possible for older children or even adults to be beginners. The target conversation goal for beginners is to be able to respond to the questions and comments of others. We keep the beginner's goals simple and easily achievable because most of the beginners will be little children.

Start by letting the beginner know he is going to learn to answer questions that others ask him. Here are the key points to teach your beginners when they are answering a question or comment directed to them.

- Look (eyes)
- Smile (mouth)
- Listen (ears)
- Answer (tongue)
    1. Loudly
    2. Clearly
    3. Slowly

First help your beginners look at the person who is speaking to them. In a survey asking what the most needed ingredients were for good conversation, one of the top answers was attentiveness. Have you found that it is hard to talk to someone who doesn't appear to be paying attention to what you are saying? Perhaps he is reading on his phone, involved with a child's needs, or simply gazing around the room.

Children have a tendency to look away from the person who is talking to them, especially if they are feeling uncomfortable. Teach your child that when he is attentive to the one who is talking to him, he is communicating value to that person. Have your children practice looking at the eyes of the person who is talking to them. Make sure they do that with you and their siblings.

While looking at the speaker, teach your child to smile. The smile communicates attentiveness, affirmation, and affection. Smiles are pleasant to the recipient and make that person feel that your child is genuinely interested in what he is saying.

ARE YOUR CHILDREN LISTENING?

Another key ingredient that helps people to have a satisfying conversation is when their conversation partner is actually listening to what they are saying. Listening goes hand in hand with attentiveness. Although a person might be listening to the conversation, if he doesn't appear to be listening, then the speaker lacks affirmation that what he is saying is being heard. In the conversation survey, some listed "not listening" as a hindrance to good conversations. They told us that to them it meant the other person wasn't interested in what they were saying.

Remind your children that when they are looking at the other person, they also should be listening carefully to what is being said. When your child is listening, he will know how to respond. If he looks away, his attention is easily diverted, and there is a greater likelihood that he will not hear what the person says.

WHAT IS YOUR CHILD'S RESPONSE?

Finally, your child needs to answer the question or comment. He will have to speak loudly, clearly, and slowly. Children have a tendency to race through their words with a high-pitched, almost inaudible, mumble. If people are always asking your child to repeat what he has said, you can be sure he needs to practice these three points of answering so the other person can understand. Practice at home, helping him with volume, speed, and enunciation.

Here is what we would expect for younger children in their conversations.

"Hi, Christy, how are you today?" Mrs. Smith asks six-year-old Christy when she sees her at church.

"I am fine, thank you, Mrs. Smith," Christy replies with a smile.

"You sure look pretty in that pink dress."

"Thank you, Mrs. Smith. It is my favorite dress. I like to wear it," Christy responds.

In this conversation, we see Christy giving more than one-word answers.

Here is another scenario typical of a conversation with a younger child.

Your child has just been introduced to one of your friends. Your friend asks your child, "What is your favorite subject in school?"

"I like history the best because I enjoy reading stories about what happened a long time ago. My history book makes history really interesting."

Recently, I (Teri) was talking to my mom and sharing this section with her. Immediately she said, "Please tell your readers to let their children answer when someone is interested enough in their children to ask them a question. So often when I try to talk to a child, his parent will answer for him rather than letting him speak for himself." Your children won't learn conversation skills if you respond for them.

IS IT POSSIBLE TO OVERCOME SHYNESS?

Overcoming shyness might be one of your greatest challenges with younger children. We don't want to confuse shyness with humility. Shyness is a fear of man. Scripture tells us, "Only fear the LORD, and serve him in truth with all your heart: for consider how great *things* he hath done for you" (1 Samuel 12:24). Even though it might be a younger child who is struggling with shyness, you can begin communicating to him the heart attitudes tied up in the shyness.

We believe, once again, that instruction and practice are the keys. Even with your little ones, talk about the importance of responding when spoken to. Discuss how that communicates love and that Jesus wants us to love one another. "Beloved, if God so loved us, we ought also to love one another" (1 John 4:11).

This is also an important time to teach your children to rely on the power of the Holy Spirit in their lives. They aren't the ones responsible for coming up with an answer to the question. The Lord will do that for them. "The preparations of the heart in man, and the answer of the tongue, *is* from the LORD" (Proverbs 16:1). Pray with the child who is shy, asking the Lord to help overcome the problem. "I can do all things through Christ which strengtheneth me" (Philippians 4:13). Spiritual teaching moments are precious. Don't miss out on them.

Make sure your child responds when spoken to within your home amongst family members. Role-play with your child situations in which others speak to him, and he replies. Do it several times a day. Make it into a little game you play if your beginner is a young child. You might put on different hats and odd glasses and pretend to be different people. Make it an enjoyable practice time.

Then broaden the practice to extended family members and friends with whom your children have the most familiarity. You could talk to the adult beforehand, explaining how you are working with your child and what you are trying to teach him. Give the adult two or three questions to ask your child that you will have had your child practice giving answers for. That way your child will have extra confidence because when the question is asked, he will know the answer.

Prepare the children ahead of time for answering questions they are asked. Don't excuse shyness. Don't even use the word! If your child refuses to speak, treat it as a discipline issue just as you would treat any other disobedience. Do not discipline in public, however, but keep the discipline for when you are at home, whether it is simply verbal correction or a consequence. If you allow a shy child to choose not to speak when spoken to, you facilitate that behavior. Their disobedience is a symptom of a heart that isn't willing to listen to you or follow you. That is something you want to address. (We recommend our book *Keeping Our Children's Hearts* for heart issues with children.)

WHAT IS A SPECIAL BEGINNER TOOL?

Many beginner conversationalists are at an age where their parents will be helping them memorize short passages of Scripture. Reciting their memorized verses to other people provides a good opportunity for the child to work on several beginning conversational skills. First, it will help with overcoming shyness. The memorized verses can be practiced until they are easy for the child to say in his home environment. Then when he is talking with someone else, he won't need to be fearful of not knowing what to say. As a parent, you can easily set up the conversation for your child like this.

"Hi, Julie. It is so good to see you. Mikey has been memorizing Philippians 4:4. Would you mind asking him to say it for you?"

"Sure. I'd love to hear Mikey's memory verses. Mikey, would you please tell me the Scripture you have been memorizing?"

When your child recites his memory verses, he will be working on speaking clearly and loudly, looking at the other person, and smiling. Almost every friend and family member you come in contact with will allow your child this opportunity to practice.

WHAT ABOUT INTERRUPTING?

While there are some children who have a hard time involving themselves in conversations, there are others who do so at the wrong time. Interrupting can be a typical, bad, childish habit. Teaching our children not to interrupt but to wait for their turn to talk at the appropriate time was difficult. We encourage you to let your children know that interrupting is wrong and why it is wrong, and to help them learn not to do it.

We found a verse that equipped us in this process with our children. "If thou hast done foolishly in lifting up thyself, or if thou hast thought evil, *lay* thine hand upon thy mouth" (Proverbs 30:32). It told our children that when they interrupt they are being foolish by lifting themselves up. It is prideful to think what I have to say is so important than I will interrupt somebody to say it. "The fear of the LORD *is* to hate evil: pride, and arrogancy, and the evil way, and the froward mouth, do I hate" (Proverbs 8:13).

We gave a consequence to a child who was interrupting of putting his hand over his mouth—"lay thine hand upon thy mouth." We only did this in the privacy of our home. Our goal was to teach our children proper behavior so that they would demonstrate it in public. If they didn't, the consequence came when we were back at home.

The hand was to be over the mouth until the parent, who had him put his hand on his mouth, released him. Generally it wasn't too long. At the appropriate time we would say, "Now there is a break in the conversation. You may say what you wanted to say."

We desire that our children would be polite, humble conversationalists. That means they look and smile at the person talking while listening attentively. They also wait until the other person is done talking before they give their response.

HOW DOES PREPARATION HELP?

I (Teri) was recently at my son's house playing with my granddaughters. The phone rang, and it was a neighbor who was moving. She wanted to bring her dogs over so the girls could say good-bye to them, and she also said she had a little gift for each girl.

I observed my daughter-in-law, Melanie, prepare the children for their interaction with the neighbor. "Girls, what do you say when someone gives you something?"

Abigail, the four-year-old, responded with, "Thank you."

Melanie looked at the two-year-old and repeated her question so Bethany could also give the correct answer.

"Good, girls, that's right. Please remember if Mrs. Morgan gives you something, you say thank you to her. What else are you to do?"

Again Abigail was the first to respond. "Look at her and smile."

"That's right, Abigail. Bethie, you tell Mommy, too, what you are to do."

Because they were so young and still learning these conversation skills, Melanie wisely prepared them for what their responses should be. You can do that as well. Discuss on the way to church or the grocery store what the children are to do when someone wants to talk to them.

WILL THERE BE EMBARRASSING MOMENTS?

Remember, when you allow your children the freedom to become good conversationalists, there will be times that your younger ones say something totally inappropriate or don't say anything at all. Expect it to happen.

Here's a story we heard that related to this. The parents had been talking to their children about modesty and dressing modestly. While grocery shopping, the four-year-old saw a woman across the aisle who was not modest and loudly asked his mommy, "Why is that lady just wearing her underwear in the store? I don't think she is modest." She was wearing a halter top and short shorts. To the child, it appeared she was just wearing her underwear.

You have your own stories similar to this, we are sure, and there will be more coming. Thank the Lord for the conversation skills your children are acquiring, and let the embarrassing moments be opportunities for humbling. After all, God gives grace to the humble. "But he giveth more grace. Wherefore he saith, God resisteth the proud, but giveth grace unto the humble" (James 4:6).

We suggest in these situations that you simply let them be for the moment. If you try to encourage your child to respond, but he doesn't, don't get upset, irritated, or angry. You might tell the other person that you are working on your child's conversation skills. You could thank them and say that they just provided a wonderful opportunity for further refinement.

Most people really don't have high expectations when they try to talk to children since so few children will respond. Wait until you are home to discuss what happened and coach your child in what he should have said or not said. Then try to give the child an opportunity to do it correctly very soon.

CAN BEGINNERS MAKE THE MARK?

Start teaching your children when they are young how to respond to those who want to communicate with them. Equip your beginner conversationalists with their tools—look, listen, smile, and answer—and let them participate in family conversation so they are prepared for that unplanned encounter with a person who wants to talk to them in Wal-Mart.

Your beginners will be the most likely to struggle with conversation shyness. This is the time to work them away from their tendencies not to be willing to talk to people. Preparation will be helpful, along with practice. You can also use your child's Scripture memory.

Set conversation expectations low for your beginners and be ready for failure. Remember that there can be as much growth from what goes wrong as there is from what goes right. In the safety of your home, failures are less embarrassing, so try to equip your children to avoid as many conversation problems as possible. However, when they happen, accept them with humility and patience, while teaching your child how to avoid the issue next time.

We believe that when you focus on teaching your children beginning conversation skills, you are setting them on a path toward conversation success. The benefits your children will gain from mastering even these beginning conversation skills are immense. It also prepares them to move to the next stage of learning conversation. Can we encourage you to put forth the effort needed to work with your beginning conversationalists?

THE PRACTICAL SIDE

IN REAL LIFE

We've only been reading your book for just about two weeks now, but while at the grocery store our oldest daughter, who is ten, showed significant improvement in her conversation skills! She was approached by a lady who was giving out samples. The lady commented on how she liked my daughter's skirt. Acacia answered back loudly and clearly, "Thank you!" The lady asked if our children were homeschooled. Acacia again replied loudly and clearly, "Yes ma'am, we are homeschooled." The lady commented on how well behaved all the children were and how she also had homeschooled her children through elementary school. Acacia then told her good-bye and to have a nice day. I was so proud of her. She spoke clearly and used her manners! After reading further, we see how she could have added to the conversation more by perhaps asking her a question, but from where we started, this is a great improvement!

BOILING IT DOWN

Teach your beginners:

- Look (eyes)
- Smile (mouth)
- Listen (ears)
- Answer (tongue)

MAKING IT STICK

Remember to take notes on each assignment, practice, or evaluation.

1. Ask your children two questions at each mealtime so that you can coach them on their conversation goals, and they can practice.
2. Plan for an extended family member or good friend to ask your child some specific questions that you have helped your child answer at home. Prepare him for the conversation.

HOW DO WE WORK WITH INTERMEDIATES?

Our whole family remembers the nine-year-old who asked for a tour of our bus. He climbed the tall steps and plopped onto one of the bench seats.

“How old is your bus?” he immediately asked.

“It’s a 1995.”

“Wow. That’s pretty old. How many miles does it have?” Question number two tumbled from his mouth.

“We aren’t really sure, because they had replaced the odometer when we got it. We are guessing it had around a million miles, and we have put another 60,000 on it.”

He continued with his conversation. "We have a small school bus that we use to get to church and do errands because there are twelve kids in our family. Our bus is a 1998, but it only has 200,000 miles. Do you drive this thing everywhere you go?"

We felt like we were talking with an adult. This nine-year-old was asking questions, supplying interesting information from his life, listening to our answers, and generating more questions. We were having a better conversation with him than we often have with adults. He was definitely in the intermediate stage of conversation.

HOW WILL THEY USE SCRIPTURE?

This is the stage to really dig into the study of Proverbs and other passages of Scripture to learn biblical instruction concerning words and conversation. Children at this stage are rapidly maturing intellectually and spiritually, so they are capable of grasping much more from your study of Scripture than when they were less skilled. Here are a few good examples:

"My tongue shall speak of thy word: for all thy commandments *are* righteousness" (Psalms 119:172).

"But I will come to you shortly, if the Lord will, and will know, not the speech of them which are puffed up, but the power. For the kingdom of God *is* not in word, but in power" (1 Corinthians 4:19-20).

"They compassed me about also with words of hatred; and fought against me without a cause" (Psalms 109:3).

Be on the lookout for these kinds of conversation gems during family Bible time. Use them to continue to refine your children's conversational skills, helping them be useful ambassadors of His kingdom.

IS ENTHUSIASM IMPORTANT TO CONVERSATIONS?

In addition to the goals presented for the beginners of looking, smiling, listening, and answering, for intermediates you can add the dimension of enthusiasm. "Rejoice in the Lord alway: *and* again I say, Rejoice" (Philippians 4:4). If that joy resides within a person, then it will shine forth in their conversations.

We live next door to Pepper, the neighbor's friendly, little mixed-breed dog. Whenever anyone comes into the vicinity of Pepper's fence, she races for the person, wagging her tail, barking happy sounds, and jumping up and down. She is so enthusiastic with her greeting that she has generated quite a following of local walkers who come prepared for their visit with a treat. Pepper has been well rewarded for her enthusiastic greetings, to the point that her owners had to put a sign on the fence asking Pepper's fan club to no longer feed her. She had developed diabetes.

We want our children to be like Pepper as they relate to and interact with people. Their eye contact, smiles, interest in the topic, and lively responses will communicate that enthusiasm to their listeners. It is a reflection of the joy of Christ in their lives.

When people sit hunched down or with their arms folded, they show a lack of interest in the conversation and certainly no enthusiasm. However, the child who is sitting up and maybe even leaning forward a bit is now indicating that he is excited about the conversation in which he is participating.

Have you been in a conversation like this with a teenager?

"Hi, Daniel, how was your trip?" Mr. McMann queries seventeen-year-old Daniel one morning at church.

"Okay."

"Where did you go?" Mr. McMann continues.

"Lots of places."

"What was the best part of your trip?" Mr. McMann keeps up his line of questioning.

"I don't know."

Contrast this conversation.

"Good morning, Mr. McMann. It is so good to see you today. How are you?" seventeen-year-old Daniel greets Mr. McMann.

"Hi, Daniel, I am doing great. How was your trip?" Mr. McMann queries.

"It was wonderful. We went to the Colorado Rockies, and I saw the most beautiful mountains, plus I was in three states I had never been in before—Colorado, Wyoming, and Idaho. Have you been to the Rockies, Mr. McMann?"

"Only once, but it was a long time ago. What was the best part of your trip, Daniel?"

"Oh, that's a hard question because we did so many great things in the midst of God's wondrous creation. I think I will say it was our family's hike to the top of Mt. Elbert. Even Mom and Libby were able to make it to the top with the rest of us," Daniel finishes.

Do you see how Daniel's greeting of Mr. McMann was the beginning of an enthusiastic "Pepper" response? Then as he answers each question with interesting information and excitement, he is going further and further for those tasty little treats that Pepper's enthusiasm earned her.

We want our children to be those kinds of people to whom others enjoy talking, and whom they know will be encouraging and responsive rather than critical and distant. Our children can be people with whom others look forward to spending time.

WHAT'S IN A NAME?

Teach your intermediate children to be attentive when they are introduced to someone and to work at remembering his name. When your child uses the person's name in the conversation, the conversation becomes more personal and meaningful both to your child and the one to whom he is speaking. Usually the other person feels a familiarity and affirmation when he is referred to by his name.

One way to help your children achieve the goal of remembering a name is to encourage them to repeat the other person's name at least three times in their conversation. Memorization is cemented through usage because what we use frequently, we remember well. If your child uses the other person's name at least three times, there is a much greater likelihood that your child will remember the name the next time he encounters the person than if he simply hears the name but never speaks it.

ARE QUESTIONS USEFUL IN A CONVERSATION?

At the intermediate stage, you can teach your child to ask questions to generate and lead a conversation. Have you seen those unique pocket knives that have several blades, a screw driver, can opener, and various other tools that open out of it? That is the type of multifunctional tool set that questions are for a good conversationalist.

The Lord Jesus was a master at asking questions. He used questions to probe for information He already knew, to test hearts, and to challenge His listeners to become spiritually discerning.

Recall with us the story of the rich, young ruler. "And when he was gone forth into the way, there came one running, and kneeled to him, and asked him, Good Master, what shall I do that I may inherit eternal life? And Jesus said unto him, Why callest thou me good? *there is* none good but one, *that is*, God" (Mark 10:17-18). Jesus knew the man's heart, and He already knew the answer to the question. However, He wanted the young man to think about what He had said.

Our children won't use questions in the same skillful manner that the Lord Jesus did. However, they can come to understand the power and potential of questions in their conversations.

Help your child avoid asking questions that can be answered by just a "yes" or a "no" unless he is planning to follow up with an in-depth question. When the child asks an open-ended question, that question will fuel a conversation much better than the one with only a "yes" or "no" answer. An example of the first would be, "Do you like brussels sprouts?" The answer will either be "yes" or "no."

Open-ended questions would be ones that ask the other person why, how, or what. Some examples would be:

How do you get along with your brothers and sisters?

What is your biggest challenge in school?

Sometimes the child could ask a question that only has a one-word answer, but then he can ask a follow-up question that is more open ended, such as:

What do you like best in school? Why?

Teach your children about asking appropriate questions. "A time to rend, and a time to sew; a time to keep silence, and a time to speak" (Ecclesiastes 3:7). They will need to be coached not to ask personal questions unless the relationship has moved into a closer friendship. Even at that, you don't normally ask things such as a person's weight, income, or what they paid for something. You don't ask them to tell you something that would not be edifying or would cause them to be critical. Learning what is appropriate and what isn't will most likely involve some failure while your children are growing in maturity and spiritual discernment.

You might have your child memorize three basic questions he could ask in a conversation and become familiar with several more. Having questions always available in his mind frees him from the fear of not starting a conversation because he doesn't know what to say. At the end of this chapter and in Appendix A are some lists of questions you could use. We think that if you brainstorm as a family, you will probably come up with many more questions to add to the list.

One family shared with us how they do this. They said they prepare their children before entering a situation where they would be expected to have conversations, such as a group gathering where they don't know many people. They encourage the children to have three conversation starters in mind. For their family, this has been very effective in helping the children feel more confident.

WHAT'S AFTER THE QUESTION?

You want your intermediate conversationalists to be able to ask questions to generate conversation. You also want them to be able to respond to questions they are asked in a manner that will continue the conversation. Let's go back to the brussels sprouts question, and observe how a good conversationalist could continue the conversation by responding with, "Yes, brussels sprouts have become one of my favorite vegetables. My mom has a way of cooking them that actually makes them taste good. I think she uses olive oil and garlic to season them. Do you like brussels sprouts?"

First you will help your child work on answering the question with more than just basic information. Show him how to give more details. The answer to whether he liked brussels sprouts was simply "yes." However, the conversation was lengthened and made more interesting by the child giving the detail of "why" concerning his taste for brussels sprouts.

Next, have your child finish what he is saying by asking a question back to the other person. The follow-up question could be on the same topic or another topic.

In our example, the child asked if the original questioner liked brussels sprouts. Depending on the answer to this question, the child could then probe with why or why not the other person does or does not like brussels sprouts. That can lead into further discussion of favorite foods and disliked ones.

Help your children practice giving responses to questions that will facilitate the conversation they are having rather than closing it down. That will mean:

1. Answer the question.
2. Give some more information.
3. Ask a question back.

Remember that there's a list of helpful questions at the end of this chapter and in Appendix A that your children could use to begin or continue a conversation.

CAN PRACTICE IMPROVE CONVERSATIONS?

Your children now have the tools, background, and teaching to make them good conversationalists. Proficiency will require the experience of jumping into the proverbial conversation swimming pool and beginning to swim.

If you purchase a special vacuum cleaner for your child and have him read the instruction manual, the vacuum still won't do any good until he actually uses it. That is what conversation practice does for your children. It allows them to utilize the tools they now have to accomplish a needed function.

The intermediate conversationalist will sometimes be able to utilize Scripture in his conversations. As you discuss Scripture during family Bible time and in daily life, you are preparing your children so that they too can insert the Word into their conversations.

We love to talk to people who have enthusiasm—a real spark of life and interest to them. Our children's conversations will be enhanced if they work to incorporate enthusiasm into their conversations. The enthusiasm should be not only for what they are saying but also for what the other person is saying. Also have them remember to use the person's name in the conversation. That draws the conversation to a more personal level.

Questions are among the most powerful tools your child has for both beginning and leading a conversation. Help him become comfortable using questions when he wants to initiate a conversation. In the midst of a conversation, it should be relatively easy for your child to come up with questions that can continue the conversation while taking it to deeper levels. As he learns more about questions, he will want to avoid questions with only one-word answers while trying to use ones that cause the other person to do more talking.

Finally for the intermediate, one of his goals will be to hone his ability to answer questions. It is relatively simple to fire off a short "yes" or "no" answer to a question, but to give more interesting and detailed information takes practice.

We can assure you that teaching your children conversation skills is a worthy investment of your time. The more you practice with them, the better conversationalists they will become. It is even possible, with the tools you are presenting to them, that they can become better conversationalists than you are!

THE PRACTICAL SIDE

IN REAL LIFE

While at church recently, my nine-year-old, Shiloh, was in the hallway, when she walked by Mrs. White.

“Hello, Shiloh. How are you doing?” Mrs. White initiated the conversation.

“I am doing very well, Mrs. White. How are you?”

“We are fine. Did you get much snow with that last storm?” Mrs. White questioned Shiloh.

“We got about six inches. How much did you get at your place?”

“Very little,” Mrs. White said.

“I really like it when it snows. My brothers and sisters and I love playing in the snow.”

This was a good example of Shiloh learning not only to answer the questions appropriately, but then to ask questions in return to keep the conversation going. Shiloh also did well in carrying on this conversation with an adult. She relayed this conversation to us since neither my husband nor I was present.

BOILING IT DOWN

Teach your intermediates:

- Use Scripture in conversations.
- Be enthusiastic. "Rejoice in the Lord alway: *and* again I say, Rejoice" (Philippians 4:4).
- Use the other person's name in the conversation.
- Start a conversation by asking questions.
- Ask a question back to the other person either on the same topic or another topic.
- Answer questions with more than just basic information. Give details.

MAKING IT STICK

Remember to take notes on each assignment, practice, or evaluation.

1. Have a family discussion to come up with basic questions that could be asked when your children are talking to other children.

2. Have at least one conversation with each child at this stage at every mealtime. Have them ask a question to begin it.
3. Ask your child a question that could be answered with just a "yes" or a "no." Then have him give you a more detailed answer and ask another question back to you.
4. Invite an extended family member, who is a believer, or a church friend for dinner. Have each person in your family participate in the conversation with the guest so that they can practice what they have learned in this chapter. After the guest leaves, have a group discussion about how everyone did.
5. Have your child talk to one older person at church each week by asking him at least two questions and trying to keep a conversation going.
6. Read through Proverbs as a family and discuss the verses having to do with conversation. Make the topic of conversation and what you can learn about it through Proverbs the special focus of your family Bible time during those days.

BASIC QUESTIONS WHEN TALKING TO OTHER CHILDREN

1. General:
    - What is your name?
    - How old are you?
    - How many are there in your family and how old?

- Tell me about your family.
- Where do you live?
- Tell me about your house.
- What are your interests?
- What do you do when you have free time?
- What activities are you involved in?
- What is your favorite thing to talk about?
- How do you most enjoy spending your time?
- Why do you enjoy that?
- Where is your favorite place to go as a family?
- Do you play an instrument? If so, what is it? How long have you played it? Why did you choose that instrument? Why do you like playing it? Do you ever play it for other people? Where?

2. Pets:
   - Do you have or have you had any pets?
   - What kind? What did you like about them/it?
   - Did you train your pet to do anything?
   - If you could have any pet, what would it be and why?
3. School:
   - Where do you go to school?
   - What do you like best in school? Why?
   - What do you like least in school? Why?

- What are you studying in school that you enjoy? Why?
- What have you learned recently that you could share with me?

BASIC QUESTIONS WHEN SPEAKING WITH AN ADULT

- What is your name?
- How many children do you have?
- Do you have grandchildren? (If an older person)
- What are their names and ages?
- Where do you live?
- What do you do for a living?
- Where do you go to church?
- Do you have any pets?
- What do you like to do?
- What is your salvation story?
- Do you homeschool your children?

WHAT'S NEXT FOR THE ADVANCED?

By the intermediate stage of conversation, your children will most likely have conversation skills that are more advanced than many adults. This isn't said to build pride but to understand how desperately these skills are lacking in society today and why it is important to work on them. They will continue to practice and hone what they have already learned, but there is more they can accomplish conversationally. It is exciting to think about the possibilities that open in our children's lives when they become skilled conversationalists.

WHEN IS IT ACCEPTABLE TO TAKE?

A real conversation involves give and take amongst the participants. It isn't a conversation if one person does all the talking. That is a lecture. It isn't a conversation if one person responds with short answers. That is an interrogation. To be a conversation, one person does some talking and then the other person responds. We introduced this topic in the last chapter with the intermediate conversation skills. Now we want to practice and refine these skills even more.

There will be different levels of give and take based on the relationship. Obviously the conversation with a stranger at the grocery store will be superficial compared to the conversation with Grandma.

In order to facilitate give and take, teach your children to look for the other person's interests or activities in which he is involved. This is a simple expression of love for another person. "A new commandment I give unto you, That ye love one another; as I have loved you, that ye also love one another" (John 13:34).

After discovering the other person's interests, your child can dig deeper into those areas through questions and comments in response to the answers. People enjoy talking about their interests and experiences.

One of our sons just flew home from a business trip to California. During his flight, he was sitting next to a middle-aged woman. Within a short time, he discovered she had a passion for her work. They had a long discussion about her high-power, well-paid position that involved setting up pharmacies, including the fact that she had worked in a pharmacy in high school but never went to college. He said it was pretty easy to discover what she liked. As soon as he asked her more about her job, she became animated and very chatty.

Help your child learn to relate any experience or information he might have on the topic being discussed. Encourage him that he participate in the conversation not simply by asking questions but by listening to the responses and then giving his personal experience with the topics. However, sometimes all one can do is to keep asking questions when the other person doesn't ask any questions in return. That was the exact experience of our son as he talked to the lady next to him on his flight. She was delighted to talk about herself, but she had absolutely no interest in him. She didn't ask our son even one question about his life. Our son stepped off that plane having learned many new things. She left without any new knowledge.

CAN YOUR CHILD LEAD A CONVERSATION?

This is also the time where your children can begin experimenting with leading a conversation in a specific direction. When our children learn how to ask questions, they have the tools and the power they need to lead the conversation. They can try to steer the conversation toward certain topics or away from others.

For example, our family doesn't watch TV, so we wouldn't care to be involved in a conversation that discusses a recent TV episode. This is what we might do.

"Hey, Joseph, did you watch that great paramedics show last night?"

"No, I didn't, Daniel. Last night I was working on a web-design project I am creating for a homeschool family that has a home business. I am doing the work for free because I need it for my portfolio and because I want to help the family's business grow. What do you think are the most important components of websites you go to? What draws you to the site, and what makes you want to buy what they sell?"

Do you see how Joseph stayed relevant to the conversation topic of last night's activities, but he led away from the movie subject? He headed the conversation in a different direction by drawing his listener to a family in need and asking for help by soliciting his listener's opinion. This should assure that the conversation will now move into website designs rather than the TV show.

Your children can also try leading the conversation to a topic in which they strongly believe. A homeschooled teen might ask the other person if he has ever heard of homeschooling and what he thinks of it. A child who has studied nutrition could ask what the person thinks are the key ingredients for good health. Every one has opinions on common subjects. The desire is not to start a debate but rather to hear what the other person has to say, with some of your child's thoughts thrown into the conversation as well.

Organized lists of question topics in your child's "tool set" for conversation will help him when he wants to lead or redirect a conversation. When he has memorized some of those questions, he won't find himself at a loss during the moment of need.

WILL YOUR CHILD'S CONVERSATION BE EDIFYING?

As our children mature spiritually, they will have the potential to be more edifying in their conversation than when they were younger. Keep reminding them to use biblical examples, draw analogies from everyday happenings to spiritual truths, and use Scripture.

We have a lady at our church whom we love to talk with because she always pulls the conversation to the Savior. She is a master of analogies, and I don't think she is really trying for those analogies.

Her heart is just so full of the Lord Jesus that those thoughts are always on her mind.

Steve called her home one day to invite her family to dinner, and she answered the phone but didn't recognize his voice. She told him he had the wrong number so he tried calling again. This time he left a voice message. The next day she said, "It was so amazing how I didn't recognize Steve's voice, but when he called back and left a voicemail, I knew right away who he was. I wonder how often I don't recognize God's voice. He is trying to tell me something, but because I don't recognize His voice, I miss it. If Steve hadn't called back and left a voicemail, we would have missed our dinner with you, just like I might miss what God wants for me if I am not listening for His voice." That was a powerful conversation!

Help your child be able to sense needs in a person's life that he might be able to minister to through Scripture, the testimony of his life or family, or simply the offer to pray. There will be times your child encounters someone who is discouraged. His words might be just what the other person needs to hear to encourage his heart. "Heaviness in the heart of man maketh it stoop: but a good word maketh it glad" (Proverbs 12:25).

Challenge your children to give God credit and praise all the time. "Praise ye the LORD. Praise the LORD, O my soul" (Psalms 146:1). Everything positive that happens in your child's life is an opportunity to praise the Lord to others. "Bless the LORD, O my soul, and forget not all his benefits" (Psalms 103:2).

One family shared with us how they do this. They have a nursing-home music ministry, and they also go to churches. When people give the children compliments regarding the talents the Lord has given them, they say, "Thank you! To God be the glory for the talents He has given me!" They also respond this way to any encouraging words people give their children.

Any trial or difficulty that your child encounters allows him to express to others his faith in Jesus and the peace that faith gives him. "Thou wilt keep *him* in perfect peace, *whose* mind is stayed *on thee*: because he trusteth in thee" (Isaiah 26:3).

CAN STORYTELLING DEVELOP INTEREST?

Real-life stories are powerful ways to capture a listener's attention and pursue a conversation. The story is generally the most accurate and interesting if it is from your own life, but you can tell other stories as well. Often a story will generate a response or questions, but if it doesn't, your child can get his listener to relate to the story by asking a question.

In our family, John is the master storyteller. He remembers details, and he makes the stories interesting. He also has the ability to mimic the characters' voices who are the key players in his story. Through his stories, he allows others to live the experience again in their imaginations after it has happened.

After returning from a business trip to California, John told us this story: "It was about midnight, and I was driving back down to Pasadena after my meeting up north. I was on I-210 and looking forward to being at my hotel. It had been a long day.

"All of a sudden, in front of me I saw a California Highway Patrol car begin weaving back and forth across the six lanes of traffic. He kept doing that until he slowed everyone down and eventually forced us to stop. Then the CHP car turned around, faced us, and pointed his spotlight on us. I was the second car back in the far left lane, just happy I wasn't in front. I kept thinking, 'What's going on? What is he doing?' Sitting on the interstate in the black of the night with a highway patrol's spotlight shining right on me was very unsettling.

"The highway patrol man then announced with his car's loud speaker, 'You are all to follow three hundred feet behind me—not one hundred, not two hundred, but three hundred feet. Do you understand? Stay behind me three hundred feet!' Then he turned his car around and began to drive slowly on.

"We followed behind, being sure to stay three hundred feet back. He was pretty specific, but it was hard to judge the exact distance. Since I was in the far left lane, I was aware that everyone who heard his instructions was staying in their lanes. The far right lane had been and still was empty. You can probably guess what happened next.

"With the slow pace of the CHP leader, a car further back on the interstate caught up with our creeping group. Seeing an open lane, he went for it, happy to get around the slowdown, I am sure.

"As soon as the highway patrol car spotted him coming in the right lane, he quickly swerved over to cut him off, almost running him off the road. The car stopped, quickly backed up, and joined the now stationary line of traffic. The officer turned around and pulled up right in front of the car that tried to get around him. He shone his spotlight on him and shouted at him through his loudspeaker, 'I told you to stay back three hundred feet—not one hundred, not two hundred, but three hundred feet! If you do that again, you WILL be ticketed! This is your final warning.'

"I imagine those first cars on the right must have felt highly vulnerable. We started off again, and a few minutes later, the CHP exited and disappeared. We all sped up and took off down the interstate like nothing had happened. I kept thinking I might see something that would give me a clue as to why that highway patrolman did what he did, but I never saw a thing."

That was a great first-person story! We asked more details about the event, and we tried to figure out why the interstate needed to be slowed down for a period of time. Was a presidential motorcade further up the road? Maybe it was a high-speed chase with which they didn't want normal traffic interfering. John's story was engaging, and it generated quite a conversation afterward.

WHAT ARE SOME STORYTELLING BASICS?

Jesus was an expert storyteller. He often gained his audience's attention by telling a story or parable. He used the parables to communicate truth He wanted them to reflect upon. Our children can also use stories as a lead-in to share truth.

For example, John might tell his interstate story to some other boys and then say, "Following the CHP officer is similar to learning to follow the Lord. I might feel the Lord telling me to do something, but I don't understand why He is telling me to do it. I need to be tuned into His voice, and if He tells me to do something, I do it."

If the story becomes too long, the listeners will lose interest in it. That means our children should learn to relate pertinent details, but leave out those that would cause the story to becoming boring.

Stories hold attention when they involve something the listener is interested in or to which he can relate. If our boys tell their grandparents a story about how they decided to purchase a computer, the grandparents probably won't stay too engaged in the story. However, if they tell a story about something cute one of the great grandchildren did, their audience's interest is piqued.

A basic story rule for children is that they understand that stories need to be accurate, not exaggerated. For younger children, they may tell a dream as a real story. They do need to learn to introduce the dream as a dream.

You want your children to learn how to share their experiences in stories with others. Especially powerful will be the stories of times when they learned to trust and obey the Lord. They will be an encouragement to others, and God will be glorified.

WHAT'S ANOTHER BENEFIT OF CONVERSATION?

One main purpose of conversation at this age is for your children to learn through the conversation. It might be something about themselves or the other person. It could be information on how to do something or how not to do it. It could be factual or emotional information. It might be useful information, or it could be information to be refuted biblically or logically.

Through conversations, a wise person can learn from others. "A wise *man* will hear, and will increase learning; and a man of understanding shall attain unto wise counsels" (Proverbs 1:5). Our children can avoid other people's mistakes, benefit from their experience, and gain from their study when they have a heart to learn. Generally the person who is sharing with them is enjoying the opportunity to allow another person, especially a young person, to glean from their knowledge.

Our friends told us that they purposefully take their children out somewhere with the sole purpose of talking to people. They have the children prepare questions in advance and determine which child will ask which questions. They have gone to hotels, post offices, nursing homes, and stores.

WHAT SHOULD CHILDREN DO BEFORE THEY SPEAK?

Some of our children have had a tendency to say whatever was in their mind no matter what it might have been. Our family has had many conversations about the importance of thinking before speaking. I (Steve) believe all of our children could tell you my saying: "Just because it crosses your mind doesn't mean it should cross your lips."

"Wherefore, my beloved brethren, let every man be swift to hear, slow to speak, slow to wrath" (James 1:19). This verse emphasizes the importance of listening so that one can put their thoughts together and properly address what was said.

"The heart of the righteous studieth to answer: but the mouth of the wicked poureth out evil things" (Proverbs 15:28). Here we find the direction not to simply pause before responding but rather to seriously think about it.

There are times when prayer is valuable before words come out. We want our children to understand the importance of relying on the Holy Spirit for answers. "But when they deliver you up, take no thought how or what ye shall speak: for it shall be given you in that same hour what ye shall speak. For it is not ye that speak, but the Spirit of your Father which speaketh in you" (Matthew 10:19-20). While these verses speak of persecution, we believe they give us a picture of the Holy Spirit providing the right words when needed if we rely on Him.

There could be some negative consequences if our children don't think before they speak. "Seest thou a man *that is* hasty in his words? *there is* more hope of a fool than of him" (Proverbs 29:20). We certainly don't want our children to speak hastily like a fool. When they take time to think and pray before they respond, they are likely to avoid the problems that come from rash words. By the time our children are advanced conversationalists, it is important that they are learning to think before they speak.

WILL THERE BE CONVERSATION FAILURES?

Just as you and I will sometimes put a foot in our mouth during a conversation, our children will as well. We can help them know when they should go back and ask forgiveness. We can encourage them when it is best to simply learn from the situation. Having a humble heart is the path to God's grace, and failure is a great teacher of humility. "... Yea, all *of you* be subject one to another, and be clothed with humility: for God resisteth the proud, and giveth grace to the humble" (1 Peter 5:5).

The more our children are willing to step into the conversation arena, the more opportunities there are not only for conversation success but also for saying something inappropriate, hurtful, prideful, incorrect, or a host of other negative things. Here is more of what

James tells us about the tongue: "For in many things we offend all. If any man offend not in word, the same *is* a perfect man, *and* able also to bridle the whole body" (James 3:2).

Our children live in the flesh and will fail in the flesh. Conversation failures can be used by the Lord for spiritual growth in our children's lives if they will submit to the teaching process. "And we know that all things work together for good to them that love God, to them who are the called according to *his* purpose" (Romans 8:28).

Often there is pain involved in the failure process, especially if hurt occurs and forgiveness is to be sought. That pain can be part of God's chastening, and it is a positive part of spiritual growth. "For whom the Lord loveth he chasteneth, and scourgeth every son whom he receiveth" (Hebrews 12:6). Be the spiritual coach to help your children through conversation failures or discouragement.

WILL YOUR CHILDREN BE PREPARED FOR LIFE CONVERSATIONS?

We believe you will be blessed as you observe your children having adult-level conversations. "A wholesome tongue *is* a tree of life: but perverseness therein *is* a breach in the spirit" (Proverbs 15:4). Their wholesome tongues will breathe life not only into your hearts, but also into the lives of those with whom they are talking.

Help them explore "give and take" in conversations and allow them experience in leading the conversation. They can learn to tell stories as they talk.

If our children have the right attitudes in their conversations, they will learn much from those with whom they speak. The wisdom they gain will have practical benefits in their lives now and in the future.

Despite their youth, our children can be used by the Lord Jesus through their conversations. "Let no man despise thy youth; but be thou an example of the believers, in word, in conversation, in charity, in spirit, in faith, in purity" (1 Timothy 4:12). Help draw their hearts to the opportunity for ministry that every conversation affords them. Words of edification are words of love, blessing, and comfort.

When your child finds himself in a difficult conversation or feels like a failure in one, encourage him in the benefits that came to him through the conversation. Then, as they say on the ranch, have him get right back up in the saddle.

Use these precious years with your children to develop their conversation skills. Be their cheerleader and ally. Be an example to them. Build your relationship with them through your frequent and personal conversations with them. We think this process of becoming skilled conversationalists will be part of making your children your best friends and making you their best friend.

THE PRACTICAL SIDE

IN REAL LIFE

After reading this book, I gave the children conversation challenges when we went to church, the nursing home, or any other public place. This Sunday we visited a church, and I asked each child to introduce themselves to someone at the church they had never met (which was most of the people since we had never gone to this church before) and have a conversation. Sunday evening we discussed the different conversations we each had. Morgan was able to introduce herself to the woman who sat behind us, and they discussed what a blessing it is to have siblings. Isaac was able to introduce himself to another woman who thanked him for singing. Isaac was then able to give God the glory for blessing him and also discuss where they each lived. Luke and Erin were able to approach two other women and tell them their names. Praise the Lord!

BOILING IT DOWN

Teach your advanced children:

- To give and take in conversation.
- To lead a conversation.
- To bring a conversation to spiritual topics.
- To tell real-life stories.
- To be a learner.
- To edify with conversation.
- To discern when to be quiet.

MAKING IT STICK

Remember to take notes on each assignment, practice, or evaluation.

1. "Here you go." Have topics written on pieces of paper and placed in a container. Pass the container to each child old enough to participate and have him pick a topic and then share immediately. This is one of the greater challenges because he doesn't have time to prepare or to hear other people's responses.
2. At the evening meal, have Dad or Mom sequentially practice with the older children "conversation hot potato." Try to keep handing the conversation back to the person you are speaking with.
3. At mealtime, assign an older child to draw out a younger person's report on his day with questions.
4. Mom or Dad engages one of the older children in a conversation. The child is to steer the conversation to another subject.
5. Assign each family member to tell a true story during a family conversation.
6. Assign a child to have an edifying and loving conversation during dinnertime, including Scripture in the conversation.

7. Invite a neighbor for dinner. Plan for the older children to take turns asking questions and leading the conversation. Evaluate after the guests have left.

   Were the words:

   - Loving?
   - Edifying?

   Did the speakers and listeners:

   - Seem attentive?
   - Have good eye contact?
   - Smile when appropriate?
   - Answer the question?
   - Give more detail?
   - Ask questions?

CHAPTER 10

HOW DO WE HANDLE ROADBLOCKS?

The previous chapters laid the groundwork for teaching your children how to be great conversationalists. As they practice and perfect their skills, they will face some challenges that we haven't yet discussed. It will help if you are prepared for these special circumstances and can equip your children for them as well.

WILL YOUR CHILD MAKE EXCUSES?

What about when your child tells you that he can't be a good conversationalist because he doesn't know what to say? Recall with us this verse from the Old Testament: "And Moses said unto the LORD, O my Lord, I *am* not eloquent, neither heretofore, nor since thou hast spoken unto thy servant: but I *am* slow of speech, and of a slow tongue" (Exodus 4:10). Moses' evaluation of himself was not God's evaluation. God had a job for Moses to do, and He was equipping Moses for that job. However, because Moses contradicted God by telling Him he wasn't capable, God gave Aaron the spokesman position. Moses missed the blessing of being able to speak for the Lord. We don't want our children to miss out on blessings.

Encourage your children that the Lord will help them with the right words when they need them. It is okay to feel inadequate. We all feel inadequate at times. However, these are opportunities to trust the Lord, allowing Him to work in and through us.

We are certain that practice will help this reluctant child. Start easy and simple. Go back to the beginner exercises. Perhaps you can give him some ideas to get him started on a few conversations. Memorizing some of the basic conversation-starter questions is important.

Another child's excuse might be that he is a slow thinker and can't come up with ongoing questions or anything else to say to keep a conversation moving. Suggest that he is putting too much pressure on himself. There are no timers in conversations, and if there is a pause while he thinks, it is all right. With time and practice, it will get better, just like it does in physical exercise. The first time you attempt a new exercise routine, it is slow and painful. By the end of the second week, it has become easier and more efficient.

Then there is the excuse that says, "I can't remember what the other person said." That is most likely a result of not paying attention to the conversation. To remember what is being said, one must be looking at the other person and concentrating on what he is saying. It is possible to be so involved in planning what we will say next that we are not retaining what is being said to us. When the pause in the conversation comes, and it is your child's turn, assure him that he will have the words he wants because he has been listening and attentive. If he doesn't, it is okay.

It could be that your children don't think they have anything interesting to share. For this excuse, you can begin prompting them to remember when something happens that would be a good conversation starter with a particular person.

For example, fourteen-year-old Jacob, with Dad's help, has just replaced an elderly neighbor's mailbox that was damaged by rowdy teenagers the night before.

"Jacob, I think tomorrow after church, Mr. Reed would enjoy hearing about how you replaced Mrs. Green's mailbox. I remember he had to replace his mailbox last summer."

"Thanks, Dad. That would be a good conversation starter for me when I see him."

"Can you think of any questions you could ask him that would keep your conversation going a bit longer after you have told your story, Jacob?"

"Well, I could ask him when he replaced his mailbox, why he had to replace it, and how he did it. Then I could ask him if he has had any recent projects he has worked on."

"Great questions, son. It's likely from those answers, you will have some more places to take the conversation. Be sure to report to me how it went after church."

"Dad, you knew I have been having trouble with what to talk to people about at church. I am glad you gave me this idea. I am excited to try it out."

ARE YOUR CHILDREN TOO PEER ORIENTED?

You may find your children gravitating to their friends for conversation and not being willing to talk to younger or older people. If this is a situation in your family, discuss it with your children. Find out why they aren't talking to anyone except their peers. Is it because they don't know what to say to people in other age groups? If so, then you can steer them toward appropriate questions and conversation topics.

Perhaps it is a self focus that indicates that the child wants to talk to his friends because he is interested in them, they in him, and he likes what they talk about. In that case, you will go back to the reason why conversation is important—to communicate love. This is where conversation drives us to discipleship with our children. We have to teach them to love others and set self aside. "By this shall all *men* know that ye are my disciples, if ye have love one to another" (John 13:35). You might encourage them to stay with you after church so you can observe how they are doing in speaking with adults.

WHAT ABOUT FILLER WORDS?

I wonder how many times our family has caught itself in the trap of habitual or filler words. These words can be distracting to a listener, and they simply have no value. However, just try to break the habit once it is engrained! We can tell you from experience, it is tough.

Here are fillers our family has had to deal with:

- Ya know
- Yeah
- Right
- So
- Ummm
- Ah
- Like

While we don't usually have all of them in our vocabulary at once, at some point we become aware of a particular word habit that has crept into our conversations. We start listening to ourselves, and we are shocked at how often we use that particular word or filler sound.

It goes something along these lines:

"We tried going over to Joseph's house, but the roads were like so slippery, it wasn't even worth trying to get there, ya know? I mean it was so bad, and I think the snow was probably like seven inches deep. The front of the car acted like a plow, ya know? So, we, ummm, turned around and came like right back."

Be aware as a family of these kinds of words and work together to eliminate them before they become entrenched. We do this by reminding the offender, which is often all of us, when he uses the word. In extreme cases, a child uses a particular word or filler so much that he can hardly talk without it. Those are even more difficult habits to break. To remind him, we will repeat the word out loud when it was said. Or we will raise a finger to make him aware without a verbal reminder. Be prepared. The child may be so distracted that he may have difficulty finishing his thought.

Also encourage your children away from using slang and street talk. Show them the importance of being ambassadors for Christ and not letting habits form by using those kinds of words.

CAN ANGER RUIN A CONVERSATION?

If someone your child is talking to becomes angry, there will likely be rash, emotion-based words spoken to him. "A soft answer turneth away wrath: but grievous words stir up anger" (Proverbs 15:1). Teach your children not to argue or respond with anger but instead to have a soft answer.

A few years ago while attending church after a conference weekend, fifteen-year-old Jesse was talking with a father. The conversation moved to the subject of college, with the father telling Jesse about his son's plans for college. Jesse entered the conversation by asking the man some questions about college and sharing why he was choosing not to go to college.

Suddenly the man became quite emotional and angry with Jesse. Jesse said the man's anger flared when confronted with why Jesse was choosing not to go to college. The logic of Jesse's no-college points shared innocently in the spirit of a typical conversational exchange sparked emotion in the dad without warning. Jesse was able to remain calm when confronted with anger.

In talking about the situation afterward, Jesse said he realized that he wouldn't have given his thoughts on college had he known it was a touchy point for the dad. He said he also gained experience in when to quietly drop a point and when to continue the exchange.

When Jesse began the conversation about college, he had no idea the hornet's nest into which he was stepping. While no parent likes to see someone become angry with his child, we do regard these as continued learning situations for our children.

If you have the option and there is ongoing anger in conversations with a particular individual, consider having your child terminate the relationship with the angry person or do it for him. "Make no friendship with an angry man; and with a furious man thou shalt not go" (Proverbs 22:24).

Somehow a nice conversation can turn into an argument when each party has differing views, expresses them, and pushes his individual point. "Only by pride cometh contention: but with the well advised *is* wisdom" (Proverbs 13:10).

Help your children learn to be careful of absolutes like "always" and "never." Children also need to be cautious of sounding like know-it-all authorities, especially with adults.

Teach them to disagree with love. Let them know that it is okay to share their thoughts and opinions, but they don't have to try to convince the other person they are right. "A fool's lips enter into contention, and his mouth calleth for strokes" (Proverbs 18:6).

Listening to the other person without arguing doesn't mean you are agreeing with him. Your child can use words like "I understand" to convey understanding of what the other person is saying without affirming him.

WHAT SHOULD CHILDREN DO WITH PRIDE AND SHYNESS?

Shy, timid, and fearful people will be very difficult to converse with. When your child encounters someone who is shy, it will remind him all the more that he doesn't want to act shy with others. If your child has struggled with shyness, he might be able to encourage the other child that he too was shy once, but God has helped him overcome it. He could share how happy he is to be beyond that shyness.

Your children will probably attempt conversations with some people who won't respond at all or who will give one-word answers. Encourage your child to be kind and loving in his attempts at conversation, but help him not be discouraged by a lack of response.

The reality is that when someone won't talk or respond, it is because of his own choice. Not speaking to someone, or ignoring them, indicates self love. Your child's appropriate response is not to be offended, but to pray for the other person, and to continue to try to break through the communication barriers.

Being in a conversation with a proud person is exemplified by his continual talking about himself in a boastful manner. "Boast not thyself of to morrow; for thou knowest not what a day may bring forth" (Proverbs 27:1). Have your children exercise caution if they have regular conversations with proud people. Pride is contagious.

WHAT SHOULD CHILDREN DO WITH INTERRUPTING AND ENDLESS WORDS?

Someone who is interrupting frequently will be difficult to have a conversation with. This can just be a bad habit, or it can be due to a serious root of pride. The result is the appearance that what they have to say is far more important than what anyone else would want to say. When speaking with an interrupter, our children's response is not to condemn but to forbear.

Our children can demonstrate love by simply letting go of their turn to talk when the interruption occurs. They can listen and speak again if the opportunity arises.

Then we have the person who incessantly talks on and on. Our children will need to be wise and willing to say very little. "He that hath knowledge spareth his words: *and* a man of understanding is of an excellent spirit" (Proverbs 17:27). It provides a great opportunity for patience, long-suffering, and kindness to be attentive and listen.

WHAT SHOULD CHILDREN DO WITH MOCKING, CRITICISM, AND GOSSIP?

Your child might find himself in a conversation that turns to mockery. A mocker is one who laughs at things and shows scorn or contempt. "Whoso mocketh the poor reproacheth his Maker: *and* he that is glad at calamities shall not be unpunished" (Proverbs 17:5). Teach your children not to participate. Why share in the chastening that the other person is going to receive?

It is also common for a conversation to involve gossip or criticism of others. You want your children to understand what gossip is. They should certainly never gossip. They should also try to kindly stop gossip or leave a conversation where it is being perpetuated. The same would hold true for criticism. One possible barometer to help your children judge what is gossip and criticism is that if they wouldn't say it to the person being talked about, then it probably shouldn't be said.

It is possible that if the mockery or gossip is occurring in a peer setting, your child might be able to encourage the group away from the wrong conversation. "*As* an earring of gold, and an ornament of fine gold, *so is* a wise reprover upon an obedient ear" (Proverbs 25:12). The way your child's rebuke is received will depend on the way it is presented and the hearts of those who hear it.

For example, a child might say something like this: "Hey, guys, I'm convicted about the way we are talking about what Danny wears. Maybe his family doesn't have money to buy him nicer things."

IS THERE A WAY TO AVOID CRUDE WORDS?

Sometimes when engaging in conversation with worldly people, they will use crude words or even curse. To forestall this, when asked how your child is doing, encourage him to respond with "blessed." Usually when someone asks us, "How are you?" most people will respond with fine, okay, so-so, or perhaps even great. If your child says, "I am blessed," immediately he has identified himself with God. Even worldly people connect blessed with religion and purity.

Teach your children to give God credit and praise all the time. This should be a natural expression from their heart's gratitude to the Lord for His working in their lives. "My tongue also shall talk of thy righteousness all the day long…" (Psalms 71:24).

Words of praise and gratitude to the Lord will tend to turn things toward spiritual topics if the other person is at all interested in such things. It will also elevate the conversation so that those who might normally use crude language will be more careful. It is a wonderful way to begin a conversation on the "right foot."

If that doesn't work, your child can interrupt the other person and explain that Jesus Christ is his Lord and Savior, and therefore, he doesn't want to hear those words. It is possible that your child might have to choose to leave the conversation.

WHAT SHOULD CHILDREN DO WITH INAPPROPRIATE QUESTIONS?

We will need to caution our children about answering inappropriate questions. Earlier we discussed teaching them not to ask inappropriate questions, but it is equally as important for them to learn not to answer them. Just because a question is asked does not mean the child has to answer. He might say, "Maybe you should ask my dad," or "I don't think that is information I am free to share."

In Matthew 4, when Satan was challenging Jesus with inappropriate statements, Jesus quoted Scripture three times and then dismissed the conversation. We aren't saying that your children should quote Scripture and then dismiss the conversation, but the example shows that inappropriate statements or questions don't have to be responded to in the way the one initiating expected. It also gives the model that our children can use of excusing themselves from the conversation or perhaps changing the topic. For example, your child could say, "It has been nice talking to you. I need to get back to my parents now."

Each family will need to decide what questions are acceptable for their children to answer and which ones aren't. It may be that they are never to tell their last name or share their address or phone number. Even with such conversation rules, there will be exceptions such as if a child is lost and needs help getting home. Who is it acceptable to give that information to and when? Some families freely discuss the price they paid for an item while other families would never share such information. Do some thinking about what your children are free to divulge in their conversations and what they aren't.

When someone is trying to trick your child with foolish questions such as "Did Adam have a navel?" or "Can God make a rock so big He can't pick it up?" that individual has a hidden agenda. "But avoid foolish questions, and genealogies, and contentions, and strivings about the law [the Word of God]; for they are unprofitable and vain" (Titus 3:9). Suggest your child change the subject since it is likely the other person is probably a mocker or scorner.

Your child could say something like, "To be honest, that's a question that one really doesn't need to answer. The most important question to be able to answer, though, is where will you spend eternity? Have you thought about that question? Do you know the answer to it?"

WHAT SHOULD OUR CHILDREN DO WITH BOY/GIRL CONVERSATIONS?

We encourage each family to discuss and set guidelines for boy/girl conversations. Some think nothing of girls initiating conversations with boys or vice versa. Others say that shouldn't be allowed until the young people are ready for courtship. Some families only want their children involved in conversations with the opposite gender once a courtship is started.

Please realize there can be dangers with boy/girl conversations. While it starts innocently, heart attachments can easily grow. That is a total unknown when the first conversations occur. Many grieving parents have come to us when a child has become emotionally and then sometimes physically involved. That could have been avoided if the family had boy/girl conversation policies in place and adhered to.

We can encourage our children to talk to those of their own gender, especially peers. They could be told to respond politely if someone of the opposite sex greets them or tries to talk to them but to not continue the conversation. Finally, you could have a policy of a girl not initiating a conversation with a boy and vice versa.

Here is an example one family shared with us of the boundaries they place on the boy/girl conversations for their family. "When we hand out tracts or do any ministry, we always pair the children. Even in business, we try to have Isaac talk with the male customers and Morgan with female customers. We know there could be danger with lengthy conversations with those of the opposite gender."

Be sure you recognize the dangers of boy/girl conversations, and then as husband and wife discuss how you want to direct your children concerning them. Give them guidelines to help implement any family policies you want to put in place concerning boy/girl conversations.

WILL OUR CHILDREN PRESS ON FOR GODLY CONVERSATION?

Share with your children your personal experiences with conversation challenges. Be determined to learn and grow right alongside your children concerning conversation challenges rather than avoiding them. Prepare them for what they will inevitably face.

Many of the conversation challenges will also challenge your child spiritually. He will be asking the Lord whether it is a conversation to excuse himself from, or he may need to pray for patience and love for the other person. He will grow in discernment concerning people and their personalities, and about when it is appropriate for him to speak versus keep silent.

Since your children will face conversation challenges, don't let those challenges be a discouragement or a deterrent to conversations. Instead make them learning opportunities that will simply hone your children's conversation skills, making them even more expert conversationalists.

THE PRACTICAL SIDE

IN REAL LIFE

1. Although we consider ourselves to be from the South, we still find it hard to understand people's speech at times. Here is a conversation we had when buying chickens at the local flea market:

   Dad: What do you feed these chickens?

   Seller: Mayonnaise.

   Dad: Mayonnaise???

Seller: No, we give 'em mayonnaise.

The last two lines of the dialog were repeated several times until it was clear the misunderstanding was not going to be resolved so we proceeded to purchase the chickens without understanding what the farmer normally fed them. Later on, we figured out the seller was saying "layer mash," but we're still not sure how to make that sound like "mayonnaise." Since then, we have learned much of the dialect and accent of the area and made many friends in the process. When we're not sure what someone is saying, we just smile and nod in polite agreement.

2. As I was washing the dishes one morning after breakfast, I was blessed to watch my son, Luke, and daughter, Morgan, walk alongside each other to care for a sick goat in our backyard. After giving the goat the medicine, I watched them walk back to the house. They were talking and smiling. I couldn't hear what they were saying because I was inside, but by the looks on their faces and their mouths moving, I could see they were enjoying each other and having a blessed conversation. When they opened the door and took off their boots, Morgan expressed her gratitude to Luke for helping her. Luke replied, "You are welcome! Praise the Lord! I am glad I could help." It is such a blessing to hear and see godly conversations among the children the Lord has blessed me with.

BOILING IT DOWN

Teach your children:

- Not to make excuses for not being a good conversationalist. (What's most important is that they are learning.)
- To talk not only to peers but also to younger and older people.
- To avoid habitual and filler words.
- Not to become angry or argue in a conversation.
- To be patient and kind in difficult conversations.
- To avoid mocking, criticism, and gossip.
- To avoid crude words.
- Not to answer inappropriate questions.

MAKING IT STICK

Remember to take notes on each assignment, practice, or evaluation.

1. Discuss conversation excuses and challenges at dinner with your children. Then discuss a plan for each event when they find themselves with that particular challenge.
    - Doesn't know what to say

- Slow thinker
- Can't come up with questions
- Can't remember what the other person said
- Don't think they have anything interesting to say
- Peer oriented
- Angry
- Proud
- Shy
- Interrupters
- Talkers
- Mockers
- Critics
- Gossipers
- Crude
- Inappropriate questions
- Boy/girl conversations

2. Make a list of habitual and filler words your family uses. Start to eliminate them.
3. Role-play some difficult conversation situations, such as talking to someone who is angry, proud, or shy.
4. Invite an unsaved person or family member for dinner. Work on conversation skills while they are there. Later have a family evaluation.

WHAT IS THE GREATEST CONVERSATION?

"Grandma, I am worried about something," seven-year-old Thomas runs across the room and hugs his grandma.

"Why, Thomas, you are way too young to be worried about anything. What is bothering you?" Grandma asks.

"I have been thinking about how Jesus saved me last month. I was so excited when I prayed and asked Jesus' forgiveness and accepted Him as my Savior. I have Jesus living in my heart now. I haven't heard you talk about Jesus saving you, though. I am worried that you don't have Jesus as your Savior and that you won't go to heaven when you die but will go to hell! Jesus died on the cross for our sins. I love you so much, and it scares me to think of you not being in heaven with Daddy, Mommy, Christie, and me. Grandma, are you saved?"

Thomas just entered into the greatest conversation of all—the conversation about the destiny of an eternal soul. Sometimes a child can approach the greatest conversation much more naturally and without the discomfort adults might feel. Not only that, but an adult will generally not react to a child who is evangelizing. At that age, there is no prompting necessary. It will simply flow from a child's heart of love and concern. That conversation with Grandma may not result in her salvation, but Thomas certainly planted some seeds. "I have planted, Apollos watered; but God gave the increase" (1 Corinthians 3:6).

IS YOUR FAMILY PREPARED TO SHARE THE GOSPEL?

As Christians, we want to be ready to share the plan of salvation. Even children can learn some basics of witnessing. If your family isn't equipped to present the Gospel to someone, you could consider taking a class at church or online as a family that teaches how to witness and present the Gospel. Doing it as a family will allow older ones to help younger ones, keep everyone motivated, and encourage family conversations about what is being learned and how it is being utilized.

When John was fourteen, we had a neighbor who was unsaved. The neighbor was a retired schoolteacher who asked John to help him troubleshoot a problem with his lawn mower. While they were working, they talked. John was able to lead the discussion to spiritual things and eventually present the whole plan of salvation. The neighbor rejected what John told him, preferring to remain an agnostic, but John knows he did what the Lord wanted him to do.

Even our children can be salt and light in a dark and dying world. "Let your speech *be* alway with grace, seasoned with salt, that ye may know how ye ought to answer every man" (Colossians 4:6). They will add power to what they say by including the Word of God, so make sure your children are prepared.

DO YOUR CHILDREN KNOW THE "GOOD PERSON TEST"?

"Hi Bob. Beautiful day isn't it?" Jim calls out.

"It sure is! I decided to enjoy it."

"I saw you sitting there. Mind if I join you?"

"Not at all. In fact, I'd like the company," Bob exclaims as he points to the chair next to him.

Bob goes to church with his wife, but over time it has become obvious to Jim that Bob doesn't have a relationship with Jesus. Jim has been praying for Bob's salvation ever since he realized that Bob wasn't saved. Today appears to be the perfect time to share the Gospel with Bob. After some small talk, Jim decides to take the plunge.

"Bob, I know you go to church, but I would like to discuss something that is a big concern of mine. May we discuss spiritual things for just a bit?"

"Hmm, Jim, that sounds a bit serious. What's on your mind?"

"Bob, I used to go to church just like you, but there came a time I realized heaven isn't a matter of just going to church. That was the best day of my life, and that is what I want to talk about. I'd like to share a few of the Ten Commandments with you and ask how you have done in keeping them. Bob, have you ever told a lie?"

"Sure I have, Jim. Hasn't everyone?"

"Bob, I have too, but that doesn't mean it is acceptable to God. God's law says, 'Thou shalt not bear false witness,' which means to lie. If we have told a lie, we have broken one of God's commandments. Have you ever stolen anything, even a paperclip?"

"Yes, I think everyone has stolen something in their lifetime."

"I'm with you on that one too. I've taken things that aren't mine, and yes, I'm guilty as well of breaking God's commandment of 'Thou shalt not steal.' Bob, have you ever coveted something that wasn't yours?" Jim continues.

"Yes, of course. Everyone has."

"I agree. I have too. I think you are beginning to see that you and I have broken God's commandments. In fact, God's Word says, 'For whosoever shall keep the whole law, and yet offend in one point, he is guilty of all.' Even if we have broken just one, we are guilty of breaking them all," Jim explains.

This is the beginning of Living Waters' "Good Person Test" method of evangelization. Living Waters is an evangelical group whose mission is to help Christians spread God's Word and to teach others to do so as well. Our family has learned the "Good Person Test," used it over the years, and really liked it. We haven't had anyone say they were offended when we have shared with them in this fashion. You can find the complete "Good Person Test" on their website, www.livingwaters.com.

Once our children were equipped with the "Good Person Test" information, we would regularly see them talking to groups of young people when we were eating at a fast-food restaurant while traveling. Some of those conversations led into the greatest conversation, while others were just pleasant communication with the goal of edification. When telemarketers call our home or we call to make an order, we will sometimes ask if they have time to talk about something off topic. If they say "yes," we start into the "Good Person Test." Doing that, we have been able to lead people to the Lord on the phone, while many other seeds have been planted.

HAVE YOUR CHILDREN HEARD OF THE "ROMAN'S ROAD"?

An easy witnessing plan for a family to learn is the "Roman's Road." The "Roman's Road" takes familiar verses, puts them together, and paves the road to leading a person to salvation. These verses are ones you want all your children to know for themselves, and they will also be profitable in witnessing encounters.

"For all have sinned, and come short of the glory of God" (Romans 3:23).

"For the wages of sin *is* death; but the gift of God *is* eternal life through Jesus Christ our Lord" (Romans 6:23).

"But God commendeth his love toward us, in that, while we were yet sinners, Christ died for us" (Romans 5:8).

"That if thou shalt confess with thy mouth the Lord Jesus, and shalt believe in thine heart that God hath raised him from the dead, thou shalt be saved. For with the heart man believeth unto righteousness; and with the mouth confession is made unto salvation" (Romans 10:9-10).

"For whosoever shall call upon the name of the Lord shall be saved" (Romans 10:13).

"Therefore being justified by faith, we have peace with God through our Lord Jesus Christ" (Romans 5:1).

"*There is* therefore now no condemnation to them which are in Christ Jesus, who walk not after the flesh, but after the Spirit" (Romans 8:1).

"For I am persuaded, that neither death, nor life, nor angels, nor principalities, nor powers, nor things present, nor things to come, Nor height, nor depth, nor any other creature, shall be able to separate us from the love of God, which is in Christ Jesus our Lord" (Romans 8:38-39).

Help your children memorize these verses and be capable of easily reciting them. Discuss as a family what each one means and when they might use them. Make sure that your children can say each of them in the correct order and give an explanation to go with it. This is a time when role-playing can be valuable. Have them actually practice saying the verses as they would to a friend or an adult. It can be easy to quote the verses to the family, but when confronted with a real person asking real questions, the verses might not be as forthcoming.

IS YOUR CHILD'S LIGHT HIDDEN?

"Neither do men light a candle, and put it under a bushel, but on a candlestick; and it giveth light unto all that are in the house. Let your light so shine before men, that they may see your good works, and glorify your Father which is in heaven" (Matthew 5:15-16). We think the best goal we could have for our children is that their lights would shine in front of others and bring glory to God. Certainly when our children can enter into the greatest conversation of all, they are letting their light shine.

"And he said unto them, Go ye into all the world, and preach the gospel to every creature" (Mark 16:15). When our children are equipped to have the greatest conversations, they are participating in the Great Commission.

Pray with your children and ask the Lord to open doors for the greatest conversation. Share with your children times when you have had the greatest conversation and times when you have tried, but it has been rejected.

Prepare your children that there will be many who are not interested in the greatest conversation and even those who despise it. "And ye shall be hated of all *men* for my name's sake: but he that endureth to the end shall be saved" (Matthew 10:22).

We truly believe that as your children become more skilled in conversation, the Lord will use those abilities as they present the Gospel to those with whom they come in contact. What greater joy could our children have than to plant those seeds for the Kingdom or actually lead someone to Christ? Make sure your children are ready for the greatest conversation.

THE PRACTICAL SIDE

IN REAL LIFE

One Sunday when we were handing out tracts, a young man asked Isaac what the tract was about. Isaac responded by saying, "This tract discusses spiritual things and talks about where you will spend eternity." The young man, Eddie, began asking Isaac and Morgan questions about their faith. Morgan and Isaac freely shared with him using Scripture and real-life examples of what Jesus has done in their lives. Eddie then told them he didn't believe God would allow him into heaven due to his sinful lifestyle. Isaac began sharing the Gospel message with sincere love and concern for Eddie. Eddie said he was not ready to make a commitment to the Lord, but agreed to pray with Isaac and Morgan and take a Bible. Isaac asked him to begin reading in the book of John and put a tract at the book, since Eddie said he didn't know the Bible well. Isaac and Morgan told Eddie that our family would be praying for him and said good-bye.

BOILING IT DOWN

Teach your children:

- Sharing about salvation is the most important conversation they can have.

MAKING IT STICK

Remember to take notes on each assignment, practice, or evaluation.

1. Plan to learn a method for evangelization as a family.
2. Practice what you are learning on each other.
3. Memorize the Roman's Road Scripture verses.
4. Look for ways to use the method outside your family.
5. Discuss as a family each opportunity, the outcome, what you were happy about in the encounter, and what you think could have been said differently.

CHAPTER 12

WHAT IS THE OUTCOME OF GREAT CONVERSATION SKILLS?

We see incredible potential for young people who will develop conversational skills in their lives. They have much to gain if they will simply grasp the value to themselves and to others of being a great conversationalist. Our job as parents is to direct them to their need, motivate them to want to learn, and then guide them in their quest to be great conversationalists.

It is easy to believe that children will simply become good conversationalists; however, we discovered that this is not true. In our personal encounters not only with young people but also with adults, there seem to be far more poor conversationalists than proficient ones.

We did a survey asking Christian families questions about conversation skills to try to determine exactly what people felt was important in a conversation and what made someone a great conversationalist. In that survey, one of the things we asked the respondents to do was to rate their conversation skills from one to ten, with one being the worst and ten being the best. The average was 7.5. That really surprised us, considering the difficulty we have in getting people to talk to us when we are at conferences.

That 7.5 average highlighted to us that it is likely most people don't even realize that there is wonderful potential for learning to be a better conversationalist. They probably don't understand what their inability to have good conversations is costing them, especially in relationships that are important to them. Of course, it is possible that only the good conversationalists filled out the survey!

DOES YOUR TEEN HAVE A BUSINESS?

Matthew has made up flyers for his lawn-mowing business and is going through his neighborhood to hand them out. He approaches a home, rings the doorbell, and an elderly lady answers it.

"Umm, I am Matthew Smith. I have a lawn-mowing business." Matthew hands the lady a flyer.

"Thank you," she responds.

That would be a fairly typical conversation for a sixteen-year-old to have with a neighbor he doesn't know. With excellent conversation skills, this is how we think the conversation might go.

"Hello, ma'am. My name is Matthew Smith, and I live two blocks over that way. I have a small lawn-mowing business, and I would like to find neighbors who need my services. Because I am young, and I can walk to the yards I am mowing, I think my rates are very reasonable. My schedule is flexible because I am homeschooled so I can schedule my work around my school and my school around my work. It is important to me to be reliable too. Do you have any interest in having me mow your yard?" Matthew says all this as he holds out his flyer.

The woman takes the flyer and says, "As a matter of fact, I have been worrying about our yard this year. My husband had a heart attack about a month ago, and he has been put on limited activity. I was getting ready to call a lawn-mowing service, but I was concerned about what they would charge since we are on a fixed income."

"Wow," Matthew responds. "That must have been very difficult to have your husband have a heart attack. What a blessing that he is still alive. I will pray for his complete recovery and for the needs you have when he still isn't feeling well. I would be happy to give you an estimate to see if it would work within your budget."

"Yes. Thank you. An estimate would be great. Thank you for praying, too. We need all the prayers we can get," the lady concludes.

This is just one example of the potential conversational skills have in the life of a young person. It might be one who wants to earn some extra income during his teen years or who is looking to start a business that can be a lifetime vocation. Those conversational skills will be valuable not only for self-employment but also for the young person who is seeking a job or wanting to do well at his place of employment.

HOW DEEP IS YOUR RELATIONSHIP WITH YOUR CHILD?

Mom and twelve-year-old April are in the car headed for an afternoon of grocery shopping and other errands.

“April, what have you been doing today?” Mom asks.

“Not much,” April replies.

“How is your piano practice going?”

“Okay.”

“What about your letter to Gram? It was supposed to be done yesterday. Is it done?”

“Not yet.”

Mom finally gives up and turns on the CD player. This conversation appears to be a dismal failure in a mother-and-daughter relationship.

However, conversations have great potential to develop and strengthen relationships. Wouldn’t you rather have a conversation that sounds like this one?

“April, what have you been doing today?” Mom asks.

“I was reading a wonderful missionary biography about Amy Carmichael. She was an amazing woman of God. Do you know she had an accident and spent many years bedridden?” April replies.

“I think I remember reading that about her.”

“Even when she was in bed, she ministered to the children who lived in her home, and she also did a lot of writing. I would love to have a heart for the Lord like she did.”

“How do you think you would get a heart for the Lord like that, April?

"I am sure it is by reading my Bible and then doing what it tells me to do. Amy Carmichael didn't complain about her pain and being bedridden even though she had frequently prayed and asked the Lord to give her mobility until she died. I know there is a verse in Philippians that says we shouldn't complain. She probably read that verse and decided she would trust the Lord even when it wasn't the way she wanted it to be. I would need to be reading like that and then living it out. What do you think, Mom?"

"I think you are exactly right, April. How is your piano practice going?" Mom asks.

"I really love it. I have one very hard piece right now that I have to make myself practice, but I know it is important for me to work on the ones that are hard. The pieces that are easier are the ones I tend to gravitate toward."

"That's a mature decision, April, to discipline yourself to practice the hard songs that your flesh tends to want to avoid. I am sure with that practice, before long it will be an easy song just like your other ones are. I'd like to hear you play it when we get home. And what about your letter to Gram? It was supposed to be done yesterday. Is it done?" Mom questions.

"Oops. I worked on it all week, and I was almost finished with it. I wanted to tell Gram about having Mr. Copen over for dinner Thursday night so I still need to add that part," April responds.

"You should do that right away so we can get it printed and in the mail."

This is a relationship-building conversation between a mom and her daughter. It grows from a daughter who has learned how to have a good conversation. These conversations draw hearts to each other.

WHAT ARE KEY FACTORS FOR GOOD CONVERSATION?

In our survey about conversation, we asked people what they thought were the key factors of a good conversation. What they told us confirmed what we already believed, and what we are encouraging you to teach your children.

Their number-one factor for a good conversationalist was that he was first a good listener. To them, listening communicated interest in the other person. Listening involved giving the speaker full attention. This included eye contact and smiling, rather than looking around the room or doing something else like texting or reading e-mail. One person described the desired quality as "being more interested in listening than on what you might say next."

Not far behind listening as a key ingredient was the ability to ask questions. It was obvious that the survey responders recognized that questions are part of what keeps a conversation moving and alive, because it was listed frequently. They suggested that a good conversationalist ask good questions, and specifically questions related to the topic at hand. One person described it as "asking relevant and significant probing questions."

The survey participants were adamant that a key factor for a great conversation is not talking too much. "Equal speaking and listening time" was an appropriate phrase we were given. Another person called it "not talking about one's self too much."

Because we desire to have others enjoy the conversations they are having with our children, it is important that we teach our children these key ingredients of good conversations. They appeared to be quite universally held. You can look in Appendix C for a full listing of what people consider to be key factors for good conversations.

WHAT ARE CONVERSATION ANNOYANCES?

As you might expect, what people on the survey said annoyed them in a conversation was the opposite of what they thought made a good conversation. For the annoyances, the top-listed one was the person who talks endlessly, especially when they are talking about themselves.

Next in the annoyance category were the topics of conversation. They didn't enjoy conversations where the other person complained, was negative, or was critical. They also didn't like hearing the person speak negatively about their spouse.

Interrupting was a huge annoyance. The interrupting meant not only normal interrupting but interrupting to finish saying what the speaker was saying. It also included letting someone else like a child interrupt.

The final one we would like to include for you is the annoyance simply in people's speech. The respondents indicated they don't like it when people talk too loudly or too softly. It is hard for them if the speaker doesn't pronounce his words clearly or drops the last syllable. They certainly didn't appreciate the use of slang or filler words such as "like" and "umm." We have lists of conversation annoyances in Appendix D so you can read them all there.

We believe that you want your children to avoid doing things in a conversation that frustrate those who are involved in the conversation with them. If you will work with your children on what we have been suggesting in this book, your children should avoid these common conversation annoyances.

WHAT IS CONVERSATION'S MOST VITAL INGREDIENT?

Perhaps the most important aspect of a good conversation is a heart that truly loves and cares for the person being talked to. Jesus Christ was the model and example of that during His time on Earth. "And the second *is* like, *namely* this, Thou shalt love thy neighbour as thyself. There is none other commandment greater than these" (Mark 12:31).

When our children truly love others, they will listen attentively to what the other person is saying. They will look at them and smile. They will choose not to interrupt, and if they are interrupted, they won't react. They will respond with an answer that is more than just one word, and they will ask questions. Those aspects of good conversation are born out of a heart of love as detailed in 1 Corinthians 13:4-6.

The selfish, prideful person does all the talking. His heart of love is self-focused love. If he lets your child say anything, he will probably soon interrupt him. Often the proud person is looking around the room for something more interesting to do than listen to your child. He might even continue reading his e-mail or be texting while your child is trying to have a conversation. Make sure your child is not the one wrapped up in the self-love that is evident through proud conversation. "A fool uttereth all his mind: but a wise *man* keepeth it in till afterwards" (Proverbs 29:11).

WHAT DOES IT TAKE FOR MEANINGFUL CONVERSATIONS?

"All my state shall Tychicus declare unto you, *who is* a beloved brother, and a faithful minister and fellowservant in the Lord: Whom I have sent unto you for the same purpose, that he might know your estate, and comfort your hearts" (Colossians 4:7-8). In these verses we see that Tychicus is going to the Colossians. He will find out about them and comfort them. It is most likely that he finds out about them through conversations, including asking them questions. Then it will be through conversations that he comforts them.

Our children will have those same opportunities to discern spiritual needs in lives and then offer comfort to those needs. "Who comforteth us in all our tribulation, that we may be able to comfort them which are in any trouble, by the comfort wherewith we ourselves are comforted of God" (2 Corinthians 1:4). Comfort that we can share with others often comes through the words of a conversation—words of love, words of sympathy, words of encouragement, words of advice, words of Scripture.

Are your children prepared for those conversations? They won't be at ease in the difficult conversations if they haven't learned the basics of simple conversations. It starts there and grows to conversations that are deep, meaningful, and even fulfilling.

HOW WILL OUR CHILDREN BENEFIT FROM BEING GREAT CONVERSATIONALISTS?

"A man's belly shall be satisfied with the fruit of his mouth; *and* with the increase of his lips shall he be filled" (Proverbs 18:20). This is a beautiful verse to encourage us that our children are spiritual winners when they have learned to be great conversationalists. Their words not only bring edification, affirmation, comfort, and fellowship to a relationship, but they also give our children a sense of satisfaction and fulfillment. Is there any price tag you could put on that?

IS THIS THE END?

When you have finished this book and completed the suggested practice exercises, is it over? Are your children done learning and implementing conversation skills? We don't think so. We believe this is a lifetime quest. Each one in our family desires to become better, more proficient conversationalists. We don't ever want to say we have arrived.

We would encourage you to make conversation skill improvement a continual focus in your personal life and then the children's. Talk about good and bad conversations on a regular basis. Encourage your children if you see them hanging back and not involving themselves in conversations. Keep in their minds the ministry opportunities the Lord Jesus gives them through their conversations. Give them meaningful purpose for the conversations they have.

WILL YOU TAKE THE CHALLENGE?

We want to challenge you to be able to say these words to your children concerning their conversation skills: "Hold fast the form of sound words, which thou hast heard of me, in faith and love which is in Christ Jesus" (2 Timothy 1:13). We believe that for these words to come true, you as the parents will have to make a determined effort to instruct your children concerning conversation.

It has been our goal in this book to equip you for the task. We hope that we have given you the tools that you need and that your success will be forthcoming. We want your children to hold on to the sound words that you share with them concerning conversation so that they can spread the faith and love of Jesus Christ.

Without a purposeful decision to make conversation skills a priority, your children might be any one of those represented in the bad conversations. What outcome do you desire for your children? What will you invest to help them achieve it?

WHAT IS OUR GOAL FOR OUR CHILDREN?

"Let the words of my mouth, and the meditation of my heart, be acceptable in thy sight, O LORD, my strength, and my redeemer" (Psalms 19:14). We want our children to be able to offer this prayer to the Lord concerning their words. We pray that the words they choose to use with others will be words that are edifying because they are spoken from hearts of love.

We think words that are acceptable to the Lord Jesus are words that fit the criteria of Philippians 4:8. They will be words that are true, honest, and just. The listener can know that he can depend on the reliability of the words he hears from our children. Their conversations will be pure and lovely, not focused on the world but on what matters with a graciousness that supersedes any crudeness. Finally, they will include good reports, virtue, and praise. That means they will avoid criticism, gossip, evil tidings, and complaining.

"The tongue of the just *is as* choice silver: the heart of the wicked *is* little worth" (Proverbs 10:20). What a beautiful picture of delightful conversation and also what a sad illustration of what comes from the heart that is wicked. Make it your goal for your children to be just and to have conversations that others will receive as choice silver.

Conversation skills may appear to be a natural outcome of living in a family and learning to speak. However, as we listen to teen conversations and even some adult conversations, it is clear that for many there is something lacking in the natural process.

We are very excited about the potential for each of your children as they learn to be great conversationalists. We believe they will stand out as dynamic personalities in the midst of a mediocre world. We think your children will build strong marriages because they know how to share their hearts, how to encourage another, and how to keep back negative words. It seems possible to us that your children will have profitable businesses built on their ability to interact with their customers and make them want to continue to do business. We anticipate your children will have the honored privilege of leading lost sinners into an eternity of joy and peace because they know how to have the greatest conversation of all.

Don't wait. Don't think it takes too much time. Don't believe it is too hard. We know you desire for your children what we are sure they can achieve with the Lord's help. Dive into this material with your children, and get going on the road to being not just good conversationalists but great ones!

THE PRACTICAL SIDE

IN REAL LIFE

I remember this conversation that my seven-year-old son had with his pediatrician seven years ago. The pediatrician said to him, "So, Luke, do you play any sports?

"No, sir."

The pediatrician queried further, "You don't?"

"No, sir," was Luke's reply.

"Oh. Well... why not? Don't you like soccer? Or basketball?" the pediatrician continued.

Once again Luke said, "No, sir."

The pediatrician looked over at me, and I was sure he was wondering why I was depriving my son of exercise, the camaraderie of team sports, and life in general. This time he addressed his question to me, "So, what DOES Luke do for fun??"

I quickly told him, "Well, Luke loves to play on our playground with his sisters, help his daddy on home-improvement projects, and he's learning to use the push mower."

Recently we were at the pediatrician's office again. Luke has matured and also been learning conversation skills. Here is the way the conversation went this time.

The pediatrician greeted, "So Luke, it's nice to see you again. What are you doing these days to pass the summer time? Playing any team sports?"

Luke, who is now fourteen, replies, "No, sir. Our family chooses not to participate in team sports, but rather to spend our time doing things that will encourage family togetherness while still getting the exercise we need. My family meets to exercise early each morning, where we do sit-ups, lunges, push-ups, and sprints up and down our driveway. Even my seven, five, and three-year-old brothers can participate with us. I try to take a walk around our property of eight acres each day with one or more of my little siblings too. Also, I love to spend my spare time helping my dad repair pianos in his shop. It's a great opportunity for me to learn the trade while spending time with my dad. And, we have a fairly large garden this summer, so I get a lot of exercise out there too. Believe me, by the end of the day, I'm physically exhausted from all the activity! Is your family gardening this year? What are you growing?"

Luke's question lead to a fruitful conversation with the pediatrician about gardening.

BOILING IT DOWN

Teach your children:

- To be good listeners.
- To be interested in the other person.
- To give the speaker their full attention.
- To look the other person in the eye.
- To smile.
- To be more interested in what the other person is saying than what they will say next.
- To ask questions, especially ones related to the topic.
- Not to talk too much, especially about themselves.
- Not to complain, be critical, or negative.
- Not to interrupt.
- Not to talk too loudly or softly.
- To speak clearly and pronounce words properly.
- Not to use filler words.
- To love others through their conversations. "And the second *is* like, *namely* this, Thou shalt love

thy neighbour as thyself. There is none other commandment greater than these" (Mark 12:31).

- Not to be wrapped up in self-love, which is evident through proud conversation. "A fool uttereth all his mind: but a wise *man* keepeth it in till afterwards" (Proverbs 29:11).

- To comfort others through their conversations. "All my state shall Tychicus declare unto you, *who is* a beloved brother, and a faithful minister and fellowservant in the Lord: Whom I have sent unto you for the same purpose, that he might know your estate, and comfort your hearts" (Colossians 4:7-8). "Who comforteth us in all our tribulation, that we may be able to comfort them which are in any trouble, by the comfort wherewith we ourselves are comforted of God" (2 Corinthians 1:4).

- That they will be spiritually satisfied with edifying conversations. "A man's belly shall be satisfied with the fruit of his mouth; *and* with the increase of his lips shall he be filled" (Proverbs 18:20).

- To discern spiritual needs and try to fill them through adding Scripture to conversations.

- To continue to improve their conversation skills.

- To have words that are pleasing to the Lord. "Let the words of my mouth, and the meditation of my heart, be acceptable in thy sight, O LORD, my strength, and my redeemer" (Psalms 19:14). "The tongue of the just *is as* choice silver: the heart of the wicked *is* little worth" (Proverbs 10:20).

MAKING IT STICK

1. Sit down individually with each child with the stated purpose to talk. Go somewhere private in the house where there won't be distractions. Tell the child you want to talk with him, and let him know he isn't in trouble. Ask your child some questions and then evaluate his conversation with you. Here are some suggestions for questions you could ask. Ask if he has anything pressing that he has wanted to talk to you about. Ask if he is having any problems in general, any problems with you, any problems with other family members. Ask him how is he spending his time.
2. After the discussion evaluate your child with the following questions. Make sure you write down your answers and any other pertinent information concerning your child's ability as a conversationalist so you can compare it to the conversation you had with your child early in this book.
    - Were you able to spend fifteen minutes talking with the child?
    - Did conversation flow between you?
    - Was it give-and-take or one-sided?
    - Was it difficult to come up with conversation topics?
    - Did your child listen?
    - Did he seem interested?

- Did he answer with a word or two or with whole sentences?
- Did he ask you questions?

3. Compare your current conversation evaluations of your children's conversations with the ones you did after the first chapter. Has there been notable improvement?
4. As a family, read through the key ingredients for a good conversation in Appendix C. Discuss these with your children.
5. As a family, read through the things that annoy people in conversations in Appendix D. Discuss these with your children.

BASIC QUESTIONS WHEN TALKING TO OTHER CHILDREN

FAMILY

- How many are there in your family and how old?
- Tell me about your family.
- Where do you live?
- Tell me about your house.
- What are your interests?
- What do you do when you have free time?
- What activities are you involved in?
- What is your favorite thing to talk about?
- How do you most enjoy spending your time?
- Why do you enjoy that?
- Where is your favorite place to go as a family?

PETS

- Do you have or have you had any pets?
- What kind? What did you like about them/it?
- Did you train your pet to do anything?
- If you could have any pet, what would it be and why?

SCHOOL

- Where do you go to school?
- What do you like best in school? Why?
- What do you like least in school? Why?
- What are you studying in school that you enjoy? Why?
- What have you learned recently that you could share with me?

VOCATION (FOR OLDER CHILDREN)

- If you could spend your life doing any job, what would that be? Why?
- What do you want to do in life?
- Why do you feel God might be calling you to that?

CONVERSATION STARTER QUESTIONS FOR ADULTS

BASIC

- What is your name?
- How many children do you have?
- Where do you live? Have you lived there all your life?
- What do you do for a living?
- What do you like to do?
- Do you homeschool your children? How long? Why?

SPIRITUAL

- Where are you going to be in a million years? Why?
- Where do you go to church?
- Why do you like it?
- Have you been saved? Would you tell me about it?

- What do you believe is God's calling for your life? Why?
- Do you read your Bible every day? Where are you reading now? Anything special you can remember from recent readings?
- What is God teaching you?
- What is your favorite verse? Why?
- Do you have family Bible time every day? How you do it?
- What person from the Bible would you most like to have a conversation with? Why?

VOCATION

- Where do you work?
- What do you do there?
- Do you enjoy your work? Why? Why not?
- What are the biggest challenges of your job?
- Do you plan to continue with this job long term?

EXPERIENCE

- What do you consider yourself the most experienced at doing?
- Where did you learn to do that?
- What was the most difficult thing you ever had to do?
- What is the best gift someone could give you?

TRAVEL

- Do you like to travel?
- Where have you gone recently? What did you do there?
- Have you ever flown on an airplane? Where did you go and why? Did you have any interesting experiences when you flew?
- When you travel how best do you prefer to get there? Why?

- Has your family gone on any interesting vacations? Tell me about them.

EMOTIONS

- What makes you happy?
- Are there times when you are sad?
- What things make you angry?

COMPUTERS

- Do you have a computer? What brand is it, and do you use it much?
- What do you enjoy using it for?
- Do you have a web site?

CONVERSATION

- Do you consider yourself a good conversationalist?
- If you were trying to teach someone how to be a good conversationalist, what would you tell them?
- What do you do when someone won't talk or barely answers your questions?

QUESTIONS FOR OLDER PEOPLE

- Do you have grandchildren? (If an older person)
- What are their names and ages?
- Tell me about your family growing up.
- Where did you live?
- What was it like when you were a little boy/girl?
- How is your health?

WHAT ARE THE KEY INGREDIENTS OF A GREAT CONVERSATION?

(A FEW PERTINENT SAMPLES TAKEN FROM A SURVEY.)

- To be a good listener and to ask good questions.
- Equal speaking and listening time.
- Paying attention and controlling emotions.
- Being considerate of the other person, reading their reactions, eye contact, a smile unless inappropriate, a focus on others, and giving glory to God.
- Outgoing personality, fun, and good company.
- Talking back and forth, showing mutual interest.
- Eye contact and a genuine interest in hearing what the other person is saying. You have to listen and not just be thinking about what you are going to say in response.
- Listen well. Think from the other person's perspective. Care about the other person. Don't just be intent on saying what you have to say and getting it out.
- Willingness to "go out on a limb" to get things going and then the ability to encourage the other person to contribute to the

conversation by listening and asking questions. Being well informed so that conversation topics are easy to find.

- Listening carefully and asking relevant and significant probing questions; acknowledge emotional cues (that seems to excite you or make you sad).
- Listening to others and responding to them in a respectful way.
- Being comfortable with silence.
- Being sincerely interested in others, not focusing too much on your fears or insecurities, learning to carry on a good conversation by talking together as a family during meals, family gatherings, or family worship.
- Listening and not multitasking by being on the phone, texting, etc.
- Showing empathy and interest in what the other talks about.
- Truly care about others and want to know more about someone.
- Enjoy talking and sharing.
- Someone who speaks truth, not gossip.
- Good vocabulary, good discernment (the Scriptures say a wise man does not tell all he knows), hospitable and friendly, engaged and active in the conversation.
- Slow to speak, thinking before speaking, and asking self if what I am about to say will be glorifying to the Lord.
- Listening as much as talking, if not more.
- Finding a common ground to talk about. Watching for nonverbal cues that the other person is actually interested in what you have to say or talk about.
- They have to like people.
- Not talking all about yourself. Turning the conversation over to the other person at the appropriate time.
- Relying on God to steer the conversation.
- Feeling comfortable with themselves.
- Finding the balance for asking questions and answering them.
- Listen to the other person and show that in your response.

- Not speaking about something you do not know about as if you did.
- Confidence that the Holy Spirit will guide you.
- Ability to remember details and names.
- It is important to consider another person's point of view.
- Not being too expressive with unsolicited opinions.
- Be friendly. Don't be overbearing.
- Ability to bridge to another topic if conversation wanes or becomes too sensitive.
- Being able to talk about issues of substance within a relatively short conversation.
- Take out your earbuds and stop doing what you are doing in order to listen and participate in the conversation—no one likes an iPod to be their competition. If you missed part of an overheard conversation because you weren't tuned in to the room or had headphones on, don't be grumpy when people get tired and refuse to repeat what you suddenly found to be interesting.
- Be willing to converse about topics that you are not expertly familiar with. Conversations do not always have to be about your pet topics. Having more than one interest in life helps. If you do know a lot about the topic that is being discussed, don't get so technical that people's eyes glaze over.
- Try to draw other people in the group into the conversation. You may have to change topics to do this.
- Speak clearly and loudly enough to be heard. It is especially frustrating for older people when they can't hear everything you are saying.
- It is important to know when the conversation needs to end (for example, when the other person needs to leave, the topic is getting too personal, the topic is getting too heated, etc.).
- Use wholesome words. If you are a Christian, speak about the Lord and all the good things He has done for you.
- Be willing to open up, not just give yes-no answers.
- Charity. True love of neighbor.

WHAT ANNOYS YOU MOST ABOUT A CONVERSATION?

(A FEW PERTINENT SAMPLES TAKEN FROM A SURVEY.)

- When people do not let you finish your thought.
- Interrupting and not really listening to what is being said.
- Complaining.
- When someone won't look me in the eye.
- They only talk about themselves and never ask about anyone else nor seem to care.
- When people are texting or playing with their cell phones when we are speaking. They are not listening at all. It's rude, but so many people do it these days.
- People talking aimlessly without thinking. People who just say what is in their head.
- People who use slang regularly in their conversations such as "like," and "do you know what I mean," repeatedly.
- Not speaking clearly.
- Interruptions.
- Lots of "umms."

- When they are obviously not listening, are looking away, or have blank stares.
- When I am speaking with someone and they turn to talk to someone else while I'm still talking.
- People talking way too much, all the time.
- It is difficult to have a conversation with a person who only values his own opinion.
- Negatively speaking about spouses.
- When they do all the talking and don't ask me questions.
- When they try to talk over someone else who is talking.
- Someone asking a question and not actually waiting for me to finish the answer.
- When people say, "Oh yeah, that happened to me too." Then they take the conversation in a totally different direction.
- Making me feel rushed.
- Being superficial. Having no depth.
- When people know everything.
- Criticism and arguing.
- When people are insensitive to others' feelings or act arrogant.
- When people feel the need to be right all of the time.
- When they are illogical and don't make sense.
- People who always turn the conversation around to themselves.
- People who constantly look around the room as if to see if there is someone more interesting they should be talking to.
- When people don't know how to dialogue. It is not enjoyable to just listen to a monologue.
- When people are very chatty as long as they are talking about themselves, but walk away when the conversation turns to me.
- When a person drops the ending of words, especially the letter "g." For example, saying "bringin" instead of "bringing."

- One-upmanship. Sometimes it is hard to speak to and hear someone who always has to "do you one better" or constantly turn the conversation to themselves.
- Poor use of grammar.
- When they speak too loudly in a raised, forceful voice.
- When the response is a grunt or "uh huh" continually rather than words.
- People who have no respect for your time, and thus keep talking even when you've stated that you need to go.
- People who stand too close to you, way inside your personal space.
- Talking with food in mouth.
- Licking lips or teeth frequently.
- When they continually allow their children to interrupt in the middle of a conversation.
- One-word answers to questions.
- Offering advice without being asked and in a "this is the way you do it" attitude.
- When speaking with a young person or teen who can't carry on a decent conversation.

STEVE AND TERI'S TESTIMONY

Growing up, Teri and I (Steve) believed that we were Christians and that Jesus was the Son of God. She was a "good girl," but I was quite worldly. She came from a fairly normal home; mine was broken. We both attended church on Sunday, but neither of us had a relationship with Jesus; therefore, it was just vain religion.

We met in college, and after marriage we felt it was the right thing to attend church together. I worked at a local radio station in between my classes and heard a pastor preach every morning at 10:30 a.m. while I was doing maintenance on the equipment. I had never heard preaching before that had such power and wisdom, so we began attending that pastor's small fellowship. Our hearts were being convicted and pulled by the Holy Spirit. At times I would ask the pastor a question and would be amazed that he didn't respond with "This is what I believe," but would always point to Scripture. He would encourage me to read the context of the passage carefully so as to understand what the writer was trying to convey. The Lord patiently continued to draw us near to Him and His Word.

One Sunday morning, the pastor was preaching on James 2:19, which says, "Thou believest that there is one God; thou doest well: the devils also believe, and tremble." Interesting—the devils believed, and we believed. I knew they weren't going to heaven, but I was planning on it. We then came to learn we were lacking a missing component that was critical for salvation. We had never repented of our sin and placed our faith in a personal Savior. The verses we shared with you in the the "Roman's Road" section of the chapter "What Is the Greatest Conversation?" were instrumental in bringing us to a saving knowledge of Jesus Christ. They pointed out our own sinful condition and the consequences of that sin. They also showed us that we couldn't ever be good enough to earn salvation.

Within a few short weeks of each other, both of us did exactly what Romans 10:9-10 says. We saw ourselves as sinners in desperate need of a Savior. Then we confessed Jesus with our mouths, believing in our hearts that God had raised Him from the dead.

We encourage you to consider for yourself whether you truly have salvation through a personal relationship with Jesus Christ according to Scripture.

MANAGERS OF THEIR HOMES

A Practical Guide to Daily Scheduling

By Steven and Teri Maxwell

- Works for families of all sizes.
- Leads in making a schedule.
- Includes hands-on Scheduling Kit.
- Filled with practical suggestions.
- Teaches how to schedule children's time.
- Contains a chapter for dads by Steve.
- Has thirty real-life example schedules.

“My schedule has given me back my sanity!! I can't believe the way my life has changed since implementing a schedule.” Tracy

“I had read almost every organizational book there was, and I still couldn't get to where I wanted to be until I applied this method!” Corrie

AVAILABLE AT TITUS2.COM

MANAGERS OF THEIR CHORES

A Practical Guide to Children's Chores

by Steven and Teri Maxwell

- Instructs in developing your chore system.
- Includes ChorePacks and supplies for four children.
- Equips parents to implement a chore system.
- Works for families of all sizes.
- Contains a chapter for dads by Steve.
- Has many helpful example chore systems.
- Allows picture chorecards to be made online.

“I can't believe how much time we have gained in our days now that we have our ChorePack system in place.” Kendra

“Its simplicity and ease of use encouraged independence and accountability at a young age.” Rachel

AVAILABLE AT TITUS2.COM

MANAGERS OF THEIR SCHOOLS

A Practical Guide to Homeschooling

by Steven and Teri Maxwell

- Written by long-time homeschool parents of eight.
- Includes practical advice for curriculum decisions.
- Shares homeschool methods that have worked.
- Contains a chapter for dads by Steve.
- Has helpful information on managing math.
- Teaches how to effectively manage your homeschool.
- Discount section in the back.

“I have learned so much from the book. The time I will save in planning for this school year is astronomical!” Jessica

“The book was well-written and thought provoking, with good use of examples to make it come alive and see how it could work for me.” Sandy

AVAILABLE AT TITUS2.COM

THE MOODY FAMILY SERIES

by Sarah Maxwell

- Fictional series/based on true life.
- Contains positive role models for children.
- Includes every day adventures.
- Homeschool family are main characters.
- Readers identify with the family.
- Popular with children of all ages.

“*My six-year-old son asked Jesus into his heart while we were reading* Autumn with the Moodys. *These books are wonderful, heart-warming Christian reading.*” *Rebecca*

“*At last, a Christian book series that is engaging and encourages my children to love Jesus more and bless their family and friends.*” *Karen*

AVAILABLE AT TITUS2.COM

REDEEMING THE TIME

A Practical Guide to a Christian Man's Time Management

by Steven Maxwell

PREPARING SONS

to Provide for a Single-Income Family

by Steven Maxwell

KEEPING OUR CHILDREN'S HEARTS

Our Vital Priority

by Steven and Teri Maxwell

AVAILABLE AT TITUS2.COM